Hoosieritis

The Contagious Condition That Is Indiana

2020 Edition

Alden Studebaker

Second Edition:
©2020 Alden Studebaker
https://aldenstudebaker.com
ISBN: 9798683851903

First Edition:
©2009 Alden Studebaker
AuthorHouse™ UK Ltd.
500 Avebury Boulevard
Central Milton Keynes, MK9 2BE
www.authorhouse.co.uk
Phone: 08001974150

First published by AuthorHouse 5/19/2009
All rights reserved.
ISBN: 978-1-4389-7074-5 (sc)

Other Books
by Alden Studebaker

Wisdom for a Lifetime in the 21st Century
How to Get the Bible Off the Shelf and Into Your Hands

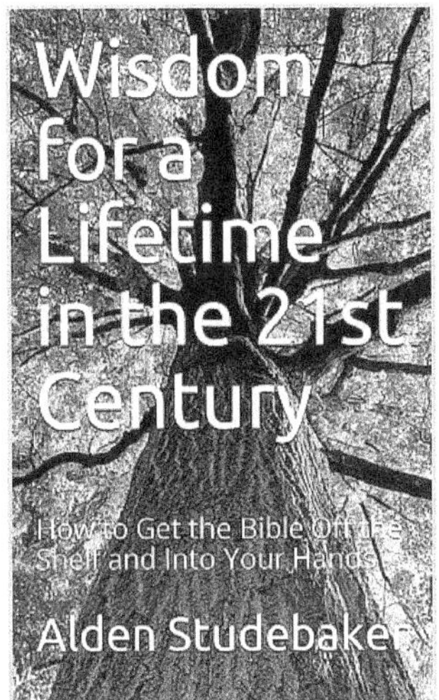

Wisdom for a Lifetime was first published in 1998 by Unity Books and became the go-to Bible handbook for students throughout the New Thought world with over 13,000 copies sold. Its purpose is to empower progressive spiritual seekers with the tools and encouragement to do their own relevant interpretations of biblical stories and passages. This second edition includes updates on the use of electronic tools that make Bible study an easier and friendlier process.

The Grid

The Grid is a novel that explores power on many levels: physical, electrical, political, economic, and spiritual. Hank Hudson is an overworked mechanical engineer from a Midwest utility. Natasha Shakhova is a beautiful Russian nuclear power plant director. Hank and Natasha meet at a European trade conference and unsuspectingly become caught up in a whirlwind of intrigue and industrial espionage. The implications for the world are staggering.

The Fault

My second novel, *The Fault,* is set in the world of seismology and Los Angeles. Alex Demurjian, a local geology professor, and Kiraz Karahan, an alluring lecturer from Istanbul, are unexpectedly thrown together. Through an intuitive sensitivity, she discovers when the Fault will slip. Can they save Greater Los Angeles from the impending peril? Will Cal's killer be caught? Along the way Alex and Kiraz experience not only the reconciliation of their ancestral past, but discover one another.

Not Just Any Bag of Bones (editor)

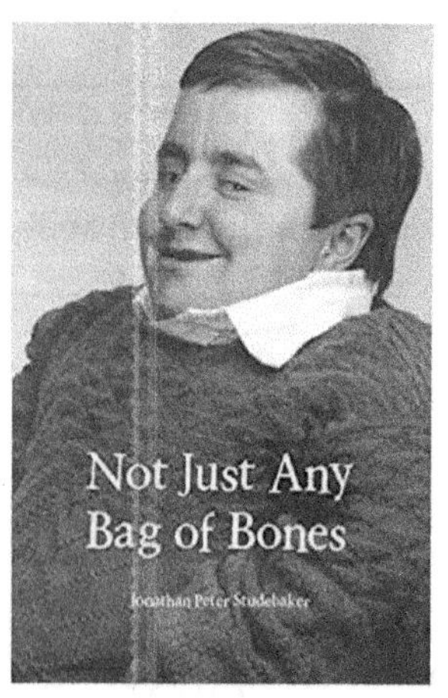

Not Just Any Bag of Bones is more than just an autobiography; it's a testament to the indomitable spirit that was Jonathan Studebaker. Throughout his life, Jonathan wanted to be a normal human being and not just another person stuck in a wheelchair. You will learn first-hand what it's like to be physically disabled and dependent on others for the living of your life. You will see through the eyes of someone who wanted access to everything able-bodied folk simply take for granted.

Author website: https://aldenstudebaker.com

Dedication

This book is dedicated to everyone fortunate enough to have been born or raised in the Hoosier State.

Acknowledgments

Although my wife and children were not born with Hoosieritis, as I was, they were all instrumental in the creation of this book:

Donna Studebaker, my wife, who continues to support me as my editor-in-chief and loving inspiration.

Jennifer Studebaker, our daughter, who helped brainstorm many of the chapter topics.

Nathan Studebaker, our son, for his technical support.

Danny Studebaker, our son, for his photographic assistance.

And, most importantly, expert, native, Hoosiers, Henry Studebaker, my father, and his brother, my Uncle Arthur, who made suggestions throughout the writing process.

Additionally, to my friend, colleague, and native Michigander, Michael Maday, who helped me with the crazy title of this book.

Table of Contents

Foreword

The seeds of this book were likely planted when I returned to my beloved home state of Indiana after a twenty-nine year absence. My wife and I had been shopping for a country home on the west side of Cincinnati, and were drawn to a ranch house in Dearborn County, Indiana.

Over the years I noticed that Indiana was indeed an interesting place in a quirky sort of way, and began to write down many of my perceptions. Finally, the spark that set *Hoosieritis* in motion happened one Independence Day. I had taken our kids to a local fireworks store to purchase snakes, sparklers, firecrackers, and my favorite explosive, bottle rockets. While standing in line to pay for our goods our daughter, Jennifer, and I, observed the vast diversity of people also waiting in line. In that moment, we realized that perhaps only in an Indiana fireworks store would you find such a variety of people from extremely divergent ethnic, socio-economic, and cultural backgrounds standing peacefully side by side. The Bureau of Motor Vehicles is probably another similar gathering. Seeing this spectacle unfold before our eyes amidst the combustible material and volatility of a fireworks store seemed even more poignant. We were all there to celebrate the Fourth of July, and we wanted only the best fireworks to accomplish our goal. Everyone in the Midwest knows that Indiana has the best fireworks. Why else were there so many Ohio license plates in the store parking lot? On the way back home Jennifer and I brainstormed many of the chapters you'll find in this book.

Hoosieritis – The Contagious Condition that is Indiana is a native son's anecdotal and comedic view of the Hoosier State. Technically speaking I am a Hoosier, although one might suggest that I'm barely one given my birthplace in East Chicago. Many Hoosiers don't consider East Chicago a true part of Indiana, but you'll have to read my chapter, *Not Really Hoosier*, to make your own determination. One might also suggest that where I've lived in Bright, Indiana scarcely passes for Hoosierland given its immediate proximity to Cincinnati, Ohio. However, perhaps living on the periphery of Indiana has provided me with the necessary objectivity to observe its unique character and report on the contagious condition that afflicts its residents

You may not agree with my commentary about Indiana, or my imbecilic suggestion that all Hoosiers are ailing from the disease of Hoosieritis. My hope and prayer is that you'll find this little book fun, interesting, and conversation provoking.

Alden Studebaker

(Isn't my last name Hoosier enough for you?)

Winter 2009

Update on the Disease

I wrote the book out of my frustration of being "hogtied" to the State of Indiana because of the educational needs of our children. All three of them wanted to attend Indiana University in Bloomington. The IU financial aid office told me that for their aid packages to remain intact my wife and I had to remain residents of the state. Thus began our extended presence in the Hoosier State, some twelve year longer than we had planned.

In all, I have lived in Indiana half of my life, so I consider myself to be a native Hoosier. I spent the other half, some ten years coming of age in Honolulu, another ten years in both northern and southern California, as well as shorter stays in Missouri, Washington, Wisconsin, Ohio, and Texas. I consider California to be my adopted home state since it's midway between Indiana and Hawai'i.

I was limited by my publisher, Author House, to twenty-four photos in the first edition. I have added thirteen more to this edition.

Things have changed in Indiana in the past eleven years since I wrote the book. Here are some updates:

- In 2013 INDOT built a fabulous bypass around the City of Kokomo, cutting the travel time on US 31 by twenty minutes. It's as if Kokomo disappeared. So, we can't call it "Stoplight City" anymore.
- In 2009 Argosy Casino in Lawrenceburg changed its name to Hollywood Casino and significantly expanded in size.
- On February 15, 2019, the Indiana Dunes National Lakeshore became the 61st national park and is now called the Indiana Dunes National Park.
- In 2011 the Seagram Distillery in Lawrenceburg was purchased by MGP (Midwest Grain Products of

Indiana) and is now called MGP of Indiana. They still make a straight rye whiskey.

- After nearly a hundred years of operation, Indiana Beach is permanently closing in 2020.
- In 2018 alcohol sales from package liquor stores became legal on Sundays, overturning a restriction that had been in place since the beginning of statehood in 1816.
- The eighth leg of the "Indiana Spider," the section of I-69 from Evansville to Indianapolis, is nearly complete. The last twenty-four miles between Martinsville and Indianapolis is scheduled to be finished by 2024.
- After completing her bachelor's degree at IU-Bloomington, our daughter, Jennifer, headed north to Purdue where she got her master's degree, proving that it is possible to graduate from both rival universities without serious mental repercussions.
- When I wrote the book in 2008 the price of a barrel of oil was $99.67. During this update in 2020 it has fallen as low as $11.26, averaging $38.13. Hence, my prediction in the book about Indiana corn solving the energy crisis has not panned out.
- A million "Hoosier State Trees" were planted since the publication of the first edition. I don't know this for a fact, but in my heart I know it just has to be true.
- Former governor, congressman and Hoosier, Mike Pence, became Vice-President on January 20, 2017.
- Finally, I am not adding "cow tipping" to this second edition no matter how many e-mails I receive. It's an urban myth about Indiana and has no relevance to the disease of Hoosieritis. I ain't gonna do it!

September 2020

Hoosier Identity

Usually the names of people, places, and things make sense. They indicate the nature of what they name, unless of course you're talking about people from the State of Indiana. The word, Hoosier, defines someone that eludes precise definition. Hoosiers are a mystery, an enigma. What is a Hoosier? Who are the Hoosiers? What the heck is Hoosieritis? Who's yer daddy? No one has ever satisfactorily defined the true meaning of the word.

As a native son of Indiana I've often wondered what it meant to be a Hoosier. People from other states, especially those that border Indiana, upon discovering that I was from Indiana, would look at me and say, "Oh, you're a Hoosier! Well, that explains it." Explains what? Is there something wrong, seriously wrong, with being from Indiana? Do six million other people and I have a disease? Do we have, dare I say it, Hoosieritis?

Thankfully, my wife, Donna, a native of Michigan, has never implied to me that I was diseased because of my birth state. I graduated from college in Michigan, and learned that most Michiganders (yes, that's what they're called, although some of them like to be called Michiganians) look down upon Indiana as that hick state to the south. One of my colleagues, a Buckeye from Ohio (and don't you think naming yourself after a tree that produces an inedible nut is a bit strange?), once described Indiana as, "that wasteland between Ohio and Illinois?" A wasteland! Come on! Indiana isn't a desert, nor was it the setting for *Mad Max Thunderdome.* Hoosiers are not laborers in methane producing underground hog farms. Hog farms, you say? Yes, Indiana has plenty of them. So, what's in a name, anyway? What is a Hoosier? What is Hoosieritis?

We could ask famous present day Indiana natives such as David Letterman, John Mellencamp, or Larry Bird what they think it means to be a Hoosier. I haven't a clue what they'd say, although it would be fascinating to hear their responses. Perhaps it's a question that every Hoosier should just ask themselves. What is the essence of my Hoosierness? When I say, "I'm a Hoosier," how does it make me feel? Questions along these lines might turn up some fascinating answers. But, where did this distinctive name come from?

There are as many theories about the origin of the word, Hoosier, as there are Hoosiers. The best one I've heard stems from the early 1800's when German immigrants populated banks of the Ohio River. The Ohio River between Indiana and Kentucky closely resembles the Rhine River in Germany. It's no wonder Germans flocked to the area. Every time my wife and I have taken a vacation to Germany I've asked her, "Why are we spending thousands of dollars to visit a place that looks just like where we live?"

During the Revolutionary War, German mercenaries were hired by the British to fight in the fledgling American country; many evidently from the region of Germany called Hessen. These soldiers were known as Hessians. General George Washington won a decisive battle against the Hessians at Trenton, New Jersey on Christmas Day, 1776. Later, as people in Kentucky looked upon these German newcomers, across the river in Indiana, they called them Hoosiers, apparently an Anglicized form of Hessian. I don't know if this is the absolute truth about the name, Hoosier, but it makes some sense. There are other theories as to the emergence of the name, Hoosier. Regardless of how the word originated, the name has stuck as a label for everyone from Indiana.

Hoosiers are an interesting breed. There have been many famous, as well as infamous, ones over the last two centuries. In addition to the previous mentioned Hoosier notables, Indiana has spawned the literary giants James Whitcomb Riley, Gene Stratton Porter, and Kurt Vonnegut; the renowned artist T.C. Steele; and aviation pioneer Wilbur Wright (his brother, Orville, was born in Dayton, Ohio). Hoosier Astronaut and Korean War Air Force pilot, Gus Grissom, flew in the Mercury program, and sadly was killed during the Apollo 1 mission. Grissom Air Force Base just south of Peru is named in his honor. Former Vice-President, Dan Quayle, hails from Huntington, where you will find his library. Racecar driver, Tony Stewart, likely began his career learning to drive on the streets of his native Columbus. Harlan Sanders, or "Colonel Sanders," the founder of Kentucky Fried Chicken, was actually a Hoosier from Henryville, Indiana, not Kentucky. Although he was a native of Kentucky, former President Abraham Lincoln spent most of his childhood years in southern Indiana.

Academy Award-winning movie director, producer, and actor, Sydney Pollack, was born in Lafayette and grew up in South Bend. Academy Award and Emmy Award-winning actor Karl Malden, grew up in Gary, and worked in the steel mills until his acting career took off. Academy Award nominated actor, Steve McQueen, was born in the Indianapolis suburb of Beech Grove. Comedian and artist, Red Skelton, began life in Vincennes. Forrest Tucker, of vaudeville and *F-Troop* fame, was from Plainfield. Former *Today Show* host and television journalist, Jane Pauley, was born and raised in Indianapolis. The actress who portrayed the mom in the TV show, *The Brady Bunch,* was none other than Dale, Indiana's own Florence Henderson. Comedian, Jim Gaffigan, although born in nearby Elgin, Illinois, grew up in Chesterton.

Musically speaking, composer Cole Porter was from Peru, and the King of Pop, Michael Jackson, may have developed his trademark "moonwalk" strutting down the streets of his hometown of Gary. His youngest sister pop star Janet, is also from Gary. Buckeye Rick Derringer, of "Hang On Sloopy" and "Rock and Roll, Hoochie Coo" fame, started the group, The McCoys, in Union City. Hoagland Howard "Hoagy" Carmichael, singer and songwriter of many popular 20th century songs, was from Bloomington. Even though she was born in Kentucky, country music star, and younger sister of Loretta Lynn, Crystal Gayle, grew up in Wabash, Indiana.

Other Hoosiers whose infamy cannot be ignored must include these personages: The poison grape Kool-Aid (it was actually Flavor-Aid) sipping Reverend Jim Jones of the Guyana cult massacre (who was a classmate of my mother's at Indiana University for a while before he dropped out) was born in Crete. Edward L. Jackson, governor of Indiana from 1925-29, was a member of the Ku Klux Klan. Jimmy Hoffa wasn't a Detroit native, but was born in Brazil, Indiana. Famous bank robber and criminal, John Dillinger, may have met his doom in an alley next to the Biograph Theater in Chicago, but he was born in the Hoosier Capital. Although not born in Indiana, John Birch, and the ultra-conservative organization named for him, was founded in Indianapolis.

However, none of these people surpasses the notoriety and stature of the patron saint of Indiana, James Byron Dean. Whatever isn't cool, hot, or hip about Indiana is completely obliterated by the ultimate Hoosier, James Dean. No other state has James Dean. Indiana claims James Dean. What state wouldn't? James Dean exuded cool, and his birth on February 8, 1931 in Marion, Indiana began the process that makes having Hoosieritis totally cool. Michiganders, Buckeyes, and Chicagoans can say all they want about Indiana being that backward, redneck, hillbilly state next door (I can't imagine people in Kentucky saying this), but they don't have James Dean. I rest my case. Driving along I-69 you can't miss the signs for the James

Dean museum in Fairmount where he spent his formative years. You'll see the blue attraction signs along with an invitation to visit the Garfield museum. Somehow I don't think a cartoon cat has enough cool to be on the same sign with James Dean, but Fairmount native, Jim Davis, would probably disagree.

If you're a Hoosier accept the fact that you are automatically cool. Pride yourself in it. Bask in your coolness. Let your Hoosierness shine. Don't be afraid to claim your Hoosier heritage. Say out loud, "I am a Hoosier, and I'm damn proud of it!" Accept the fact that you are riddled with the incurable disease of Hoosieritis. James Dean had it, and he blazed the trail for us so that we Hoosiers could all be cool in spite of our being a rather weird, kooky, and strange bunch. He cinched the deal. We're Hoosiers. And, if you're not a Hoosier, you are welcome to move to Indiana and become an honorary Hoosier, just like Abe Lincoln. Talk to my wife, the Michigan native, who made the conversion. You too may catch the contagious condition that is Indiana!

Hoosier Places

Spend a little time driving around Indiana, or peruse a map of the state, and you will observe that the disease of Hoosieritis has caused people to label their towns, cities and other features by some rather unusual and thought provoking names. For instance, why is South Bend in the most northern part of the state? This has never made any sense to me. The logical explanation could be that the St. Joseph River makes a southerly bend through South Bend as it swings back north into Michigan, but couldn't they have come up with a better name for the place? I just think that if you're going to name a city with the word "south" in it the city ought to be in the southern part of something, that's all. Of course, how to do you explain that North Bend, Ohio is in southern Ohio? I'll let a Buckeye answer that question.

My bet is that someone from Michigan gave South Bend its name. Perhaps Michigan could annex South Bend and then it would be in the most southern part of Michigan. Michiganders, unlike Hoosiers and Buckeyes, obviously know how to name places correctly since Southfield, Michigan is in the southern not northern part of their state. A campaign called the South Bend Michigan Coalition could be formed to push for the change. But, this kind of radical reapportionment of territory could lead to war between Indiana and Michigan, and then what would be done about the several miles of the Indiana Toll Road that go right through South Bend? You couldn't call it the Michigan Toll Road because it's in Indiana. Michigan doesn't have any toll roads, and the idea of paying to drive on a road goes against the grain of most Michiganders. Scrap the South Bend, Michigan idea. We just have to accept the strange fact that South Bend is in northern Indiana.*

We Hoosiers also have to make our peace with another odd labeling fact: that Michigan City is not in Michigan, but in Indiana. Whose brainchild was this? Okay, perhaps we can justify this name because Michigan City is close to Michigan (another Michigan annexation possibility), and is located on Lake Michigan. But are we Hoosiers so ashamed of our state that we couldn't have named it, for instance, Indiana City? Iowa and Pennsylvania have towns named Indiana. There is an Indianola, Indiana, but that's hardly unique, or distinctive, since there are Indianolas in California, Florida, Georgia, Illinois, Iowa, Mississippi, Nebraska, Oklahoma, Pennsylvania, Texas, Utah and Washington. There's an Illinoi, Indiana right on the state line with Illinois. We didn't have any trouble using a neighboring state's name for a town, now, did we? However, there is no Indiana or Indiana City, Indiana. There is Indianapolis, but that's a whole other chapter (see *Hoosier Capital*).

Please, don't get me wrong about liking Michigan City, Indiana. I have many fond memories of being taken to the Washington Park Zoo by my grandmother. My eldest sister, Bonnie, was born in Michigan City. Sadly, her ashes are scattered on Mount Baldy, a sand dune near Michigan City. It's just that one would logically surmise a town called Michigan City would be in Michigan, not Indiana.

Head straight south about seventy miles from Michigan City and you will come to a place that proudly wears the name Indiana, Indiana Beach. Indiana Beach is the Hoosier State's largest amusement park, and is perched on a spit of land in the middle of Lake Shafer, a lake created from the waters of the Tippecanoe River. But, hold on there a minute, what's a place called Indiana Beach doing in the middle of the state and not on a real beach, like is found in

Michigan City? You would think that if you were going to a place that was called "beach" it would be at a real beach on a significant body of water. Get out a map of Indiana and ask yourself where would you put a place called Indiana Beach? Would you put it in the middle of an agricultural sea of corn and soybean farms in White County? I don't think so! Look to the northwest corner of the state and you will notice a rather large body of water called Lake Michigan. There are even a few towns along its shore with beach-like names such as Long Beach, Beverly Shores, Ogden Dunes, and Dune Acres. Heck, I wouldn't be surprised if the sand at Indiana Beach was brought in from Michigan City.

I say, let's push for a name change. Indiana Beach should donate its name to Michigan City, and then adopt a new, flashier name, such as Hoosier Water World or Aqualand Indiana (there are several Aqualand theme parks in Europe, why not Indiana?). In exchange for its new name, each spring Michigan City (now called Indiana Beach) would bring in several truckloads of Lake Michigan sand to replenish the beach at the park. It's only fair when you consider what a win-win situation it is for all concerned. Michigan City sheds its confusing name, and we resolve the question of why Indiana Beach isn't anywhere near a real beach.

Care to guess how many towns in Indiana are green? There's Green Acres, Greensboro, Greenbrier, Greensburg, Greencastle, Greendale, Greenfield, Greens Fork, Green Hill, Green Oak, Greentown, Greenville, Greenwood, and if you like alternative spellings, there's a Greene. Count 'em, that's fourteen! Granted, some of these places are just wide spots in the road and others are full-fledged cities, but they all tout to be green something. All of them by virtue of being in a humid climatic zone are green at least six months of the year. That's unavoidable. It rains a lot in Indiana, which cause plants to grow, greening every place in the state whether its name includes green or not. Even Brownsburg is green during the growing months of the year.

You would think that these towns could do more to promote their greenness. Greensburg has a tree growing out of the top of its courthouse; they've got the green thing going. However, take for example Greentown, a small, inconspicuous village smack dab in the middle of Howard County. You would miss Greentown on most trips unless you were trying to get from I-69 to Kokomo on US-35. If you take this ride what you'll notice about Greentown is what little effort the townspeople have put forth to live up to their city's name. One would expect a place called Greentown to be very, very green…houses painted green with green roofs, green gutters, and a greenhouse in every backyard. All lawns would be mowed with unmistakably green John Deere tractors or Lawn Boy push mowers. The entire downtown should sport a green motif, with green lampposts, green pavement, and green traffic signals. City hall would be decked out in green (and not just the doors), fire trucks would be florescent green, and all police cars would be green and white with green lights atop. The official drink would have to be Mountain Dew and its variants, the greenest of all the soft drinks. The official fruit would be the lime, and how about a nice evergreen like the white pine as the official tree. The official logo would be the shamrock. The Jolly Green Giant would volunteer to be the town mascot and would show up each fall for the Green Festival to celebrate the harvest of the official apple of Greentown, the Granny Smith. There's still time for Greentown to put itself on the map as a destination, rather than just another place to blast through on the way to somewhere else.

Speaking of green, let's take a look at the town of Greencastle located about fifty miles west of Indianapolis, and home to DePauw University. My question is simple, "Is there a green castle in Greencastle?" Or, how about New Castle, a small city just south of Muncie. Is there a new castle (or was there ever a new castle) in New Castle? Is there any kind of castle in Castleton, a northeast Indianapolis neighborhood? There are no green castles in Greencastle, and there never was a new castle in New Castle, but there actually is a castle in Castleton. In France it would be called *Chateau Blanche.* Here in the good ole U.S.A. we simply call it White Castle, home of the famous "slider" steam cooked hamburger. You'll find Castleton's White Castle located on 82nd Street near Allisonville Road. Finally, a place that lives up to its name!

Those who have been fortunate enough to travel to Europe have likely seen a castle or two. Although no true castles were ever built in the Hoosier State one cannot deny the strong resemblance between Indiana's brownstone county courthouses and European castles. These impressive buildings lord over the towns they inhabit with a castle-like architectural swagger. My favorite is the Fulton County courthouse in Rochester (see *Hoosieritis Photos*). Maybe there are castles in Indiana after all.

Indiana seems to have a fascination for places ending with the letter, "O." Twenty miles up the road from Greencastle is Amo, which in Latin means, "I love." I wonder if the residents of Amo know that. Maybe they are a loving folk. Northwest of Lafayette there's Fargo. Fargo is not a big place, nor is Toto, a wide spot in the road between Knox and North Judson. This name could be referring to the total of some items, as *in toto*, or, it could have been named after Dorothy's yappy little dog from the *Wizard of Oz.* My money is on the dog, but I could be wrong. Ask someone from Toto. Maybe they know.

The Irish rock star, Bono, may not be aware that he has two Indiana places that wear his name. One Bono lies along the East Fork of the White River deep in Lawrence County, and the other Bono can be found in Vermillion County near the Illinois state line. Maybe he'll perform a concert at one of these locales someday. Another musical "it ends in O" place is Disko, located on SR 114 where Fulton, Miami, and Wabash counties converge. Disko is claimed by Wabash County, and sadly, for the dance inclined, there are no discos in Disko. Maybe somebody should build one.

Another musical and largest of the "it ends in O" places, is the city of Kokomo. The Beach Boys song back in the 80's talked about going "way down to Kokomo," but they weren't singing about this small city in the middle of Howard County. For most Hoosiers, other than the forty-six thousand residents of the city, Kokomo is one of those places you must endure. Why? If you've not driven through Kokomo on US 31 allow me to explain this comment with one simple word. Stoplights. When the US 31 bypass around the city of South Bend was built they at least had the sense to make it a limited access freeway. You can zip around South Bend at sixty-five miles per hour without ever having to brake for a stoplight. However, if you're traveling through Kokomo, welcome to your brake pedal!

Kokomo calls itself the "City of Firsts," because it's the place where the first car was invented by Elwood Haynes in 1894. Add to that claim of firsts the first highway bypass that bypasses nothing, but takes you past everything! For some brilliant reason the US 31 bypass around downtown Kokomo was deliberately and intentionally made into the most hellish piece of roadway for anyone attempting to simply drive through. You just don't drive through Kokomo, you crawl through it. Truckers call it, "Stoplight City." It's as if the Chamber of Commerce conspired to force every traveler to stop in Kokomo for lunch, and maybe even breakfast and dinner too, because it feels like it takes all day to get from one end of town to the other. If you were hungry driving into Kokomo and drove out hungry, it's your own darn fault. If you were looking for haute cuisine, maybe you'll have to go to Indianapolis, but the nine miles of four-lane divided stoplight infested highway running through Kokomo must have more franchise restaurants per lineal mile than any place in the United States. One of the few Cracker Barrel restaurants not located on an interstate freeway is in Kokomo. The city just screams, "Stop, and eat." You might as well. You're gonna have to stop at the next light. I guarantee it.

Other "it ends in O" places include Mexico, a small town in Miami County just off of the aforementioned US 31. How many Mexicans live there? There's Cuzco, a tiny little place next to the Hoosier National Forest in DuBois County. How many Peruvians call it home? There's a Modesto in Monroe Country. How many Californians have transplanted themselves there? There many other "it ends in O" places to discover and ponder: Ashboro, Banquo, Bobo, Cato, Como, Marco, Mongo, Otisco, Owasco, Rego, Saltillo, Tampico, Waco, Wellsboro, and Yeddo.

My favorite "it ends in O" place is Churubusco. Anyone traveling on US 33 between South Bend and Fort Wayne will go through Churubusco. Churubusco is quite a mouthful to say. Sometimes it's just called, Busco. What do you call a native of Churubusco? A Churubusconian? A Churubuscovite? A Buscoer? It's a tough call. The town was originally two towns, Franklin and Union. Franklin was on the north side of the railroad tracks, and Union on the south. In 1847, when the towns were large enough to apply for their own post offices, they were required to apply for a single post office. The names Franklin and Union had already been used as names for towns in Indiana, and so a new name was selected. Churubusco! The name was suggested to honor the American victory at the battle at Churubusco, Mexico during the Mexican-American War. Ole!

Naturally, not every interesting and strange place in Indiana falls into the "it ends in O" category. Hoosieritis can keep any Hoosier up into the wee hours wondering about questions like: Do Hoover and Kirby have the best-vacuumed homes in the state? Is the sun always shining in Daylight, or, are there stars in Starlight? Do people drive fast in Speed? What's the favorite snack food in Popcorn? Can one find a quiet place in Solitude? Do they speak English in English, or French in Frenchtown? Does Fountain have any fountains? What's for lunch in Chili? Are any clean-shaven men in Beard? Speaking of beards, does Saint Nick own a house in Santa Claus? What does a deck of cards contain in Spades? Is Buddhism the primary religion in Buddha? Is everybody right in Correct? Do people put their hands in their vests in Napoleon? Is the police department busy in New Harmony? Can a man find a bride in Groomsville? Is there a copy of *The Republic* in Plato? Is road kill a popular dish in Raccoon? Do profits abound in Windfall? Are people getting ahead in Progress or Advance? Is everything cheap in Economy? Are there posh resorts in Leisure? Do they tell tall tales in Story? Can you say, "You can bet your sweet bippy," in Bippus? Are bean burritos on the menu in Gas City? Whew! Do they pump oil out of the ground in Petroleum? And, what's scampering across the floors in Roachdale?

Honestly, I have no idea what to make of Loogootee other than it's an ordinary southern Indiana town with a very unique name. Of course these questions are rather inane, even I must admit. But, Hoosieritis is a disease of the crazed. I just figure that a place and its residents ought to reflect their names in some small way. For instance, I live in Bright. So, it makes perfect sense to me that I consider myself to a bright person, both in disposition and intelligence, because I live in Bright. Just ask my wife, the Michigander. She lives there too.

Like many states, the names of trees are also popular Hoosier places, including: Ash Grove, Beech Grove, Burr Oak, Cherry Grove, Elmdale, Hemlock, Lone Tree, Mulberry, Maple Valley, Sassafras, Pines, Walnut, Willow Branch, and just plain Forest. I am happy to report that all of these trees grow quite well in Indiana. God help us Hoosiers if we had called a place Palm Springs or Coconut Grove! And, like many states, Hoosiers have borrowed well known place names from other states and countries. Indiana has its Albany, Atlanta, Austin, Boston, Buffalo, Charlottesville, Cincinnati, Cleveland, Dayton, Denver, Galveston, Houston, Lincoln, Memphis, Miami, Nashville, Raleigh, Rochester, Santa Fe, Sitka, Topeka, Washington, and Wheeling. Internationally speaking, there are Algiers, Berne, Dover, Geneva, Georgia, Mecca, Montpelier, Morocco, Moscow, Ontario, Paris, Rome, Scotland, Shanghai, Siberia, Sparta, Vienna, Warsaw, and Waterloo. None of these rival the originals in size and stature, but they're Hoosier places nonetheless.

It must be noted that Hoosieritis causes Indiana natives to pronounce the names of places, shall we say, uniquely. La Paz, meaning "the peace" in Spanish, is a small town on US 31 literally a stone's throw north of US 6 in Marshall County. Most people outside of Indiana would call it, La Paz, like the Oz in the Wizard of Oz, and as it is pronounced in Spanish speaking countries. Hoosiers call it La Paz, as in jazz. Maybe it should be re-spelled, La Pazz. Head back south down US 31 to Carmel, an upper middle class Indianapolis suburb. Non-Hoosiers mistakenly pronounce it Carmel. They accentuate the name "Mel" on the end of the word, like the well-known city where Clint Eastwood was mayor. Nope! Hoosiers pronounce Carmel as if it were a chewy piece of candy. Versailles, the county seat of Ripley County, is not pronounced by Hoosiers like the famous royal chateau and city just outside of Paris, France.

Hoosiers prefer to end the word as if you were asking, "What ails you?" From Versailles, continue east on US 50 a few miles then go north on SR 101 to Milan, home of the legendary 1954 state high school championship basketball team. What's interesting is that locals do not pronounce Milan like the Italian city from where it likely derived its name, but with the accent on the first syllable and a long "i." Don't forget to say it with a southern Indiana twang too. Smile when you say, Mi-lan.

Let's shoot back up to northern Hoosierland for a moment to the small towns of Shipshewana and Nappanee. These towns are synonymous with the word, Amish. Of course the Amish aren't unique to Indiana. Significant populations of Amish also live in Pennsylvania and Ohio. Enter these towns and you'll see where the 17th and 21st centuries collide. Hummers drive alongside horse drawn buggies. Incidentally, Hummers are assembled just down the road in nearby Mishawaka. It is interesting that these two Amish communities (and Mishawaka) have distinctively Native American names, rather than more Germanic names that would reflect their population. Perhaps it's because the Amish live close to the earth like the Native Americans did, but then, it could be just a coincidence.

Any book called *Hoosieritis* would be incomplete without mentioning the most interesting named place in all of Hoosierland – French Lick. Minnesota may have a French Lake, and Missouri, French Mills. Both New York and West Virginia have a French Creek. California has a French Gulch, but no other state has a French Lick. How did French Lick ever get its name? The story is told that mineral springs in the area attracted animals that came to lick the salt covered rocks. The French were the first Europeans to settle the area. "Voila!" French Lick! In the mid-1800's a hotel was built and French Lick became a spa town.

Considering its small size (less than 2,000 inhabitants), French Lick has attracted some famous visitors over the years including Al Capone, Irving Berlin, Joe Louis, and Franklin Delano Roosevelt. However, French Lick is probably most famous for its hometown son, basketball legend, Larry Bird. Today, French Lick sports a brand new Vegas-style casino.

*South Bend was originally called, St. Joseph's and Southhold. Interestingly, the area was once part of Connecticut, which ceded the land in 1786. It became part of the Northwest Territory the following year. In 1800 it became part of the Indiana Territory, and then in 1805 was swallowed up by the newly formed Michigan Territory. In 1816, when Indiana achieved statehood, it became permanently Hoosierized.

Hoosier Values

When most people think of Indiana, and the Midwest in general, the term "family values" often springs to mind. It's not that family values don't exist in other places around the world, indeed they do. People everywhere want to do what's best for the benefit of their families. As we look at any given day in Hoosierland we can easily observe these essential human values being expressed. Drive by a country home on a summer weekend and if you notice cars parked all over the lawn you can bet that cousins have gathered for a family reunion. Sunday mornings you'll notice families filling the pews of Hoosier churches all across the state. Minivans and SUV's can be seen darting around Hoosier communities as children are chauffeured from soccer practice to music lessons. You'll see people pitching in to help one another in need, whether it's mowing their neighbor's front yard, or helping to build a Habitat for Humanity house for a homeless family. This is Hoosieritis in its highest expression. We give our full attention to what we truly value.

What do Hoosiers also value? Spend some time in Indiana and you'll observe a couple of things. Like many people, Hoosiers for better or worse worship the Almighty Dollar. A case in point, casino gambling. The proliferation of casinos along the watery edges of Indiana is a phenomenon that cannot go unnoticed. State licensed "river boat" casinos dot the Hoosier shore of Lake Michigan and the northern side of the Ohio River sucking mammon from fellow Hoosiers and residents of neighboring state's metropolitan areas. Ohio River boat casinos in Lawrenceburg, Rising Sun, and Vevay (pronounced Vee-vee), Elizabeth, and Evansville pick money from the pockets of people from Cincinnati to Louisville to Owensboro.

Lakeside casinos in Hammond, East Chicago, Gary, and Michigan City exact their toll on Chicagoan's and Michiganders disposable income. For all of the touting of basic Midwest family values Hoosiers have no trouble enabling their neighbors, both Hoosier and Non-Hoosier, by feeding their addiction to games of chance.

Of course, Indiana is not alone in the pursuit of gambling dollars to fill public and private coffers. Las Vegas, Reno, and Atlantic City come to mind as gambling meccas, and there are many other states that have legalized gambling. Indian casinos on reservations have become a lucrative way for the remaining native American population to receive some recompense for the numerous broken treaties and forced migrations exacted upon them by the U.S. government over the past two hundred years. Interestingly, of Indiana's neighboring states, only Illinois and Michigan offer casino gambling. Kentucky and Ohio have none as yet. All of these states represent potential money to Hoosier gambling facilities.

Some may find my commentary on Indiana's casino gambling harsh. After all, a certain slice of the profits go directly to the state and local municipalities to fund public projects and services, not to mention the many jobs casinos create for Hoosiers. During my tenure as the minister of a Cincinnati church I witnessed both the so-called benefits to the public and their drawbacks through three members of my congregation, one of them a Hoosier. I'll leave out their names to protect their privacy. They were all women, one in her sixties, one in her forties, and the other in her thirties. The senior of the three was the clerk-treasurer of one of the aforementioned casino cities. She was the Hoosier. Prior to the arrival of the casino the annual budget of her city was around five million dollars, about right for a small city of its size. Suddenly, with the arrival of the riverboat casino, the city's annual revenue increased exponentially to over fifty million dollars! I would often visit her office where casino checks in the amount of hundreds of thousands of dollars would be laying on her desk ready for deposit. One would think that having all of this money would be a boon to any city. Can you ever get too much money?

Money has a way of making people crazy. My dear church member was old school. Rules and propriety were meant to be followed and not bent for personal and political purposes. For years she constantly challenged local politicians over their alleged abuses and feather nesting plans for the money she controlled. We would often see her on the evening news quixotically battling these self-serving windmills as she tried to keep city hall honest in its financial dealings. Eventually the electorate swept them all out of office and installed a new group. I saw this as a relief to her, but it was clear to me that the extra layer of stress the casino money created had taken its toll on her well-being.

The woman in her forties was a blackjack dealer at a casino. Prior to the opening of the casino I saw her in church quite regularly, but once she began working there her attendance became significantly less frequent. Her shifts on the boat often included late Saturday nights making it difficult to attend Sunday morning church services. Thankfully for the church, she was a faithful financial supporter. Apparently working at a casino benefited her financially.

The woman in her thirties was a young mother, and a volunteer in our church nursery. My wife and I enjoyed the many conversations we had with her about our families and raising kids until one day she told my wife she was leaving the church. Why, we wondered? Was she moving out of town? What had prompted her to leave? The reason: Because the church's social events committee was sponsoring an excursion to a casino. Unbeknownst to us, her husband was a gambling addict, and she strongly felt that a church group shouldn't be going to a casino. We told her that the excursion didn't actually require going into the casino. Participants could simply go to the bargain priced buffet and go home afterward (which is what we did since gambling isn't our thing). Even given this rational explanation, she was adamant in her position and did indeed leave the church. We were completely powerless to do anything to stop her departure.

For better or worse, each of these women was impacted by the presence of casinos in Indiana. For one it required constant vigilance to ensure that casino funds be invested and utilized properly, for another it was her livelihood, and sadly for one, it was a place of destruction for her family. There is no doubt that the State of Indiana and its casino municipalities benefit from their business. Heck, all of the roads in Dearborn County where we live are now paved, including my once favorite dirt road, Scenic Drive. I used to love flying up and down this hilly road watching the dust fly all over the place. But, no more! It's paved, but paved because we Hoosiers decided that making money by allowing games of chance on our soil is acceptable and desirable.

Maybe we're saving people the long flight to Vegas, or the long drive to Mississippi or Missouri where many casinos await them. That's a convenient justification, allowing the convenience of doing one's gambling locally, pun intended. If people are going to gamble, they'll find their way to a casino somewhere. Perhaps Indiana is simply performing a civic duty to the people of Illinois, Kentucky, Michigan, and Ohio by having casinos strategically located near their borders. If these states aren't going to provide sufficient gambling opportunities for their citizens, then we Hoosiers must pick up the ball and run with it. Place your bets.

One thing you'll observe about the Hoosier State is that it has the largest and greatest number of fireworks stores anywhere in America. Cross over into Indiana from any neighboring state on a major road and you will discover that Indiana is the "right to blow yourself up" state. Why all the fireworks stores along the state lines? Same reason there are Hoosier casinos. There's money to be made. A certain percentage of the general population loves fireworks, but most states won't allow the sale of really good fireworks. Indiana fireworks stores are noted for being stocked with the best explosives God and China ever made.

It has become a tradition in our family that every Fourth of July we go to one of the several fireworks stores near our home and purchase a modest amount of goods. Sparklers and snakes for the kids, and firecrackers and bottle rockets for dad – that's me! I must admit, I'm horribly addicted to bottle rockets. I have a twenty-inch long steel pipe that I set up in our driveway at just the correct angle to pepper our large front yard with bottle rocket refuse like they were mortar shells. I like to shoot off one after another – light the fuse, drop it in the pipe, and whoosh they fly up in the sky for a hundred of feet, then bang! It's a yearly pyromaniac's delight that feeds my Hoosieritis affliction.

You'll notice at these warehouse-sized fireworks stores that well over half of the cars in the parking lot have out of state license plates. Since we live near Cincinnati we see mostly Ohio plates. As with casino gambling, there's a downside to fireworks sales. Fireworks are DANGEROUS! They are, after all, explosives. They explode. You have to be eighteen to buy fireworks, but not all eighteen-year olds are qualified or smart enough to handle explosives. Every year people lose body parts and sometimes their lives by mishandling fireworks. Indiana fireworks are so good that it's not always necessary to drive to a park on the Fourth of July to observe a public fireworks display. Although we live in a rural area, we can easily observe our neighbors' private fireworks shows a half-mile away.

Another moneymaking venture Hoosiers engage in is inexpensive alcohol retail outlets. We're not talking about fuel grade ethanol, but the kind of alcohol you drink. Cheap Indiana liquor stores seem to proliferate near state lines. When my father lived in Michigan, he would frequently stop at a drugstore in Indiana and pick up a case of cheap beer for about seven bucks, something he couldn't do in Michigan given the ten-cent per can deposit there. I spent years trying to talk him out of drinking cheap beer, posing the question, "How many beers do you think you have left in you?" Now he mostly drinks imported Dutch beer, but occasionally he sneaks back over to that drugstore and buys some of that cheap swill.

Not far from my house is the small Dearborn County town of West Harrison. If you drive northbound on State Road you are in Harrison, Ohio, and southbound puts you in West Harrison, Indiana. Telephone numbers in Harrison start with 367, and in West Harrison it's 637. There is a liquor store on the West Harrison side of State Road with signs up touting their low prices and vast selection. You never see signs like that on the Ohio side of State Road. Never. What is most interesting about this willingness to supply all those over twenty-one with adult beverages is the simple fact that state law prohibits the sale of package alcoholic beverages on Sundays. If you want beer for the Sunday afternoon NFL football party at your house, and forgot to buy it on Saturday, you're out of luck. Better go to Ohio or some other state. This same prohibition also extends to the hours the election polling places are open in Indiana. We Hoosiers feel that a drunken electorate is a bad one. God forbid that we have any drunken voters marking their ballots! Are you out of beer on the first Tuesday in

November? You'll have to wait until after 6:00 p.m., or back across the state line you go. That's Hoosieritis for you!

In fact, what makes Dearborn Country veritably ooze with Hoosieritis values is its extreme aspects. First, it has one of the longest riverboat casinos in the country. Second, it's home to the largest distillery in the country. Third, it has the longest ski slope in the State of Indiana. Fourth – it has the largest fireworks store this side of any river you can name. Yes, Dearborn County, Indiana has it all! You can lose all your money at the casino, wash away your depression drinking local liquor, and either do a Sonny Bono to yourself on the ski slopes, or blow yourself up with explosives. I caution anyone from taking this self-destructive course of action, but the elements of such an experience exist right here in Indiana.

If you really want to get down to what makes Hoosiers tick, what gets them up in the morning, what they love and value above all things, it's basketball. Basketball, not Christianity, or any of the other world's spiritual paths, is the true religion of the Hoosier State. Basketball is a severe form of Hoosieritis. In front of nearly every Hoosier home you will find what my Hoosier uncle calls, the "Indiana Phallic Symbol. No, we won't go there! We're talking about a basketball hoop. It could be standing alone on a pole with a matching backboard, or tacked up to the side of a barn or garage. Mine sits in the front yard with a redcedar trunk for a post (see *Hoosieritis Photos*).

The sacred pole and hoop are worshipped by Hoosiers beginning at a young age. Kids learn the litany of shooting the orange ball through the hoop as if it were an altar to the Most High, while dreams of being the next Larry Bird (who played his college ball at Indiana State University) or Isaiah Thomas (who played at Indiana University) dance through their minds. Indianapolis' WIBC, the News and Talk of Indiana, 1070 AM, not only covers the NBA Indiana Pacers games, but also video broadcasts of high school basketball games on its website. Indiana is serious about basketball. It's not just a casual interest, but a statewide religion.

Hoosiers like other sports too. The Indianapolis Colts are a top notch NFL team, having won Super Bowl LXI in 2007. But for high school athletes, the ultimate goal is the state basketball finals. In the chapter, *Hoosier Places*, I mentioned the town of Milan, which was the home of the legendary 1954 state high school championship basketball team. During that season this small town team managed to work its way to the state finals and win. This story inspired the movie, *Hoosiers,* starring Gene Hackman and Dennis Hopper. If you have not seen this movie, buy yourself a copy TODAY! Do not rent or stream it, buy it! That's your assignment! Basketball is to us Hoosiers what God is to the rest of humanity. This movie is fraught with Hoosieritis, and explains the reason why basketball is the state religion of Indiana.

Hoosier Capital

During the broadcast of an NBC Sunday Night Football preseason game between the Seattle Seahawks and Indianapolis Colts, while the camera panned the downtown lights of the Hoosier Capital, premier play-by-play announcer, Al Michaels, described Indianapolis as a "very vibrant city." Without a doubt this is true. Indianapolis is Indiana's most vibrant and sophisticated city. It is the hub around which the entire state revolves whether it involves commerce, government, or culture. It is a city that lives up to its name, the city of Indiana.

Indianapolis is a major league city, not only with the 2007 Super Bowl Champion NFL Colts on board (who stole into town from Baltimore in 1984), but also the NBA Indiana Pacers. Hoosier native Larry Bird coached the Pacers during the 1997-2000 seasons, and former Indiana University star and Detroit Piston, Isaiah Thomas, coached the Pacers from 2000-2003. Kids around Indianapolis wear Colts' quarterback Peyton Manning's No. 18 and now retired Pacer Reggie Miller's No. 31 Pacers jerseys in abundance. Although not a major league team, the Indianapolis Indians AAA baseball team has its supporters. The Indiana Fever, WNBA team plays in the Hoosier Capital. The NCAA has its headquarters and Hall of Champions in Indianapolis. Many NCAA final four basketball games have been held in the city. Sports are big business in Indianapolis, and I haven't even mentioned the biggest annual sporting event the city hosts. Keep reading.

Indianapolis has developed attractions that you simply won't find anywhere else in Indiana. The Indianapolis Zoo touts the Dolphin Adventure Dome, the first fully submerged underwater dolphin viewing experience, hence saving Hoosier families the expense of driving to Florida to see these amazing sea mammals. Indianapolis is also home to the world's largest children's museum where you can walk with the dinosaurs in the Dinosphere or be transported into space in the SpaceQuest planetarium. It must be noted that dinosaurs never set foot in the Hoosier State during their one hundred forty million-year reign on earth, nor has anyone been taken up into space from Indiana soil, although I'm sure there have been some UFO abductions on record. Dolphins and dinosaurs in Indiana? Why not? Just because they're not specifically Hoosier dolphins or Hoosier dinosaurs doesn't mean that we Hoosiers can't enjoy seeing them, does it?

As a young child growing up in northwestern Indiana we rarely thought about the Hoosier State capital. As described in the *Not Really Hoosier* chapter, this part of Indiana is dominated by a rather sizeable nearby non-Hoosier city. Indianapolis was the place where my uncle, aunt, and cousins lived, and we rarely went there. They would usually drive up to our house for visits at the family's ancestral home. We called Indianapolis, "Naptown." Why? Because we were lazy? Let's face it, it's easier to say "Naptown" than "Indianapolis." Indianapolis is a mouthful, a total of six syllables. Naptown is easier to write it too, seven letters instead of twelve. Since we weren't from Indianapolis, we could use the slang expression without any repercussions. Of course, Naptown implies that Indianapolis is a city worthy of a nap, that is, nothing interesting ever happens there, but we know this to be a falsehood. Indianapolis has got the Colts, the Pacers, dolphins, dinosaurs, and that yet to be named big annual sporting event. It's coming in the next paragraph.

The other shortened version of Indianapolis is Indy. Lots of people use this word in place of the more cumbersome, Indianapolis. Compared with Naptown, Indy has only four letters. Hence, the Indy 500, the more conventional way of referring to that one event of the year when millions of car racing enthusiasts around the globe are focused on the Hoosier State. You can say, the "Indianapolis 500," but that sounds pompous and arrogant. Just say, Indy 500. Naptown 500 doesn't have the right ring to it. But then, the Indy 500 isn't even held in Indianapolis. The fabled Brickyard raceway is located in neighboring suburban Speedway. Do you think Speedway 500 sounds better? Nah.

Anyone who has actually driven in Indianapolis has experienced the *real* Indy 500, and we're not talking about that famous car race every May. No, we're talking about Interstate 465. Truckers have called Indianapolis "Circle City" for years. Why? Some might postulate that the reason for this label has to do with Indianapolis' downtown Monument Circle, but a more likely explanation is because I-465 circles the city in an almost perfectly rectangular…circle. Many cities have similar belt freeways that encircle the outer edges of the city's limits. Nearby Cincinnati, where I've lived, has its I-275. Washington, D.C. has its Beltway, or I-495. Le Boulevard de Périphérique defines Paris. The A10 Autobahn, or Berliner Ring, encompasses Berlin. The M25 motorway encircles greater London. I've been on all six of these circular freeways. Nothing beats the "Indy I-465."

The posted speed limit on I-465 is fifty-five miles per hour, but don't let that fool you. The only time anyone drives fifty-five on I-465 is when one of Naptown's finest happens to be using the roadway on their way to an urgent call or lunch break. The rest of the time, and that's 99% of the time, think Indy 500. Think foot to the floor and go like hell. Stay out of the left lane lest you be run over by one of Naptown's Mario Andretti wannabees. If you were to drive I-465 for a full five hundred miles, just like the Indy 500 racers, you need to make nearly nine laps around its fifty-seven mile circumference. At fifty-five miles an hour you would be driving for over nine hours from start to finish. However, at seventy-five weaving in and out of traffic like the typical Indianapolis speed demon, you could cut the drive down to just under seven hours. This doesn't allow pit stops for fuel, food, and going to the restroom. Perhaps someone could start a tradition of driving I-465 for the full five hundred miles, an unofficial Indy 500, with the winner receiving a trophy, a free lawyer, and bail money to get out of jail after the Indiana State Police catches up to them. Maybe the I-465 version of the Indy 500 isn't such a good idea after all.

Speaking of I-465, if you were to take a road map of Indiana, focus your eyes on Indianapolis, then squint a little, what would you see? Try it for yourself. Can you see it? Can you see the spider? One of my sons, who'll remain nameless to avoid his embarrassment, is deathly afraid of spiders. No spider lives long within his personal space. Yes, he is very fond of his adopted home state of Indiana. If he only knew that it is constantly held in the clutches of this ferocious arthropod!

Back to the map. If you gaze at the map looking for this gigantic arachnid it will literally jump out at you. Notice that the Hoosier Interstate freeways all connect with the semi-roundish body of the spider, otherwise known as I-465. Indiana is covered by a large seven-legged spider! Two legs are I-65, two more are I-70, an additional two are I-74, and a final leg is I-69. But, don't spiders have eight legs? Indeed they do. So, why doesn't the "Hoosier Spider" have eight legs? Did one get pulled off? The answer is this: the eighth leg hasn't even grown yet, or, should I say, been built.

The proposed extension of I-69 through southwest Indiana is in the planning stages and is plagued with a heap of "not in my back yard" controversy. Apparently no one wants the eighth leg of the Hoosier spider draped across their property, nor do Indiana residents want to pay for this extra appendage. What is wrong with us Hoosiers? Can't our Hoosieritis overcome our Interstate arachnophobia? Just across the state line in the Commonwealth of Kentucky preparations have been made to use the Western Kentucky Parkway as an extension of I-69. What are we Hoosiers waiting for? Kentucky is ready. For the time being, State Route 37, which trails off of the I-465 spider body and terminates in Tell City on the Ohio River will have to suffice as the eighth leg of our Hoosier Spider. Eventually the good citizens of the Hoosier State will figure out how to extend I-69 down toward the Bluegrass State.

Indianapolis is also known for being the only major US city that is not on a major waterway. You have to admit that the White River, which flows through the heart of the Hoosier Capital, isn't much of a river. But this exclusive claim of being the only large city not on a significant river or body of water is simply not true. I can imagine that the residents of Phoenix, the capital city of Arizona, a city of millions, might have something to say about this unique status. The Salt River that flows through the Valley of the Sun isn't much of a river either. In fact, it's usually devoid of water most of the time and there are some roads that actually go through the riverbed. Can we agree that any river you can drive through isn't much of a river? At least no Indianapolis streets go through the bed of the White River. We may have Hoosieritis, but we're not crazy.

Hoosier Education

Any discussion of Hoosier higher education must begin with Indiana University and Purdue University. This statement is not intended to take anything away from Indiana's other post-secondary institutions of higher learning. Butler University, the shining star of Indianapolis, has a reputation for being one of the top liberal arts colleges in the Midwest. One might assert that Notre Dame University is the cultural heart of South Bend, not to mention that they usually field a formidable football team, and is near the home of the College Football Hall of Fame. Ivy Tech is Indiana's community college, with campuses dotting the entire state. Indiana State University in Terre Haute is perhaps best known as the college of basketball great, Larry Bird. Ball State University in Muncie boasts that it has the nation's best wireless campus. I can attest to this claim.

Our daughter, Jennifer, attended the Indiana Academy for Science, Mathematics, and Humanities, a residential high school for gifted 11th and 12th grade Indiana students located on the Ball State University campus. When she began her Indiana Academy education she was issued a laptop computer and began her addiction to wireless high-speed Internet. Back home on "the farm" all we had at the time was slow-speed dial-up. Our backward internet service certainly cramped her style on those required monthly weekends at home, but somehow she survived. When she entered college at Tulane University and complained bitterly about their lousy internet I wondered if she should've simply enrolled at Ball State.

Having violated my own assertion that Indiana higher education must start with Indiana and Purdue Universities, let's move on to that discussion. Indiana University, with its main campus located on nearly two thousand acres, in the hilly, wooded southern Indiana city of Bloomington, is perhaps the most picturesque college campus in the country. Limestone, cut from nearby quarries, was used to construct many of the university's buildings. IU, as it's usually called, is known for its exceptional business, law, and music schools. Eighty-three foreign languages are taught at IU including Lakota, Norwegian, and Uzbek. How many colleges offer that vast a selection?

Although IU has a stellar academic reputation, over the years it has been consistently rated by the *Princeton Review* as a top party school, and in 2002 took top honors. To quote my Purdue University engineering school graduate father, "IU, that's a country club. Purdue is the salt mines." It's amazing that my parents ever hooked up at all given that my mother was an IU grad. Perhaps he was just bragging about his degree being well earned and that my mother's was scholastically inferior. I think he was just bragging.

Earlier I mentioned that our daughter attended Tulane University. Like IU, Tulane has a national reputation for excellence in education, and our daughter had received an abundance of financial aid to attend there. Hurricane Katrina did not heavily damage Tulane, but the effects of the storm have had a lasting impact on New Orleans. Jennifer's freshman class, Tulane's first post-Katrina class, was much smaller in size than previous ones. I'll never forget the university president's address, at a gathering of new students and their parents, where he commended everyone for putting their faith in the university to take care of their children's education and safety. I drove away from the Crescent City feeling very good about leaving her in the capable hands of the Tulane University faculty, staff, and police department.

There is another interesting parallel between Tulane University and Indiana University. Many college students consider them both to be good party schools. Tulane is especially known as one of the top schools for the use of hard liquor, and is just a few miles from the famous French Quarter and the street named for hard liquor, Bourbon Street. Lindsay Lohan had one of her binges at "The Boot," a bar just off campus.

One day Jennifer informed us that although she enjoyed her classes and was getting good grades she would be leaving Tulane at the end of the semester and transferring to Indiana University. Whoa! Hold on here! What happened? Why was she leaving this prestigious private school to attend the "state school?" We were mystified by her decision. Given her strong academic bent we knew she wasn't simply trading one party school for another. We pondered her decision for months until we finally realized that there was only one plausible explanation: Hoosieritis.

That's right, Hoosieritis, the malady that afflicts those who call the Hoosier State home. She had been overcome by Hoosieritis; the contagious condition that is Indiana. She heard the siren call, "Back home in Indiana..." What else could it be? Although Jennifer isn't an Indiana native, having been born in southern California, the ten-plus years of living in Indiana had completely eradicated her Golden State roots. The other "ends with iana" state could hold her no longer. Sorry Louisiana, Jennifer came home to roost in her beloved Indiana. At least our son, Nathan, learned from his sister's experience. He accepted his Hoosieritis affliction, and aimed his higher educational intentions directly toward Indiana University without a detour to an out of state school.

Head north from Bloomington about a hundred miles and you'll arrive at Purdue University, or, the salt mines, as my father calls it. Purdue is a land grant school located in the small city of West Lafayette on a bluff above the Wabash River. Architecturally speaking, when compared with the aesthetically pleasing old-world looking limestone campus of IU, Purdue is more modern, and decked out mostly in basic red brick. Don't get me wrong, Purdue's campus has its charm, but it's just not quite as artistic as IU. The architects who designed Purdue's buildings might want to take me to task on this point, but when you have one of the top engineering schools in the nation, form is not nearly as important as function. Purdue's mascot's name, the Boilermaker, and we're not talking about an alcoholic beverage, is very descriptive of many Purdue students. Some graduates of Purdue have literally become boilermakers, my father among them. For the latter part of his engineering career, my father, Henry, has been the top boiler expert for the United States Navy. Whenever a boiler had a problem at a naval base anywhere in the world, my father would be on the next plane to that location. "The Legend," as his Navy comrades called him, was probably the oldest employee to have served the Navy, retiring at the youthful age of eighty years old. As a Purdue Boilermaker, my father knows his way inside and around a boiler like Larry Bird knows his way around a basketball court. When I needed to understand the functioning of the boiler at my church in Cincinnati, I didn't call in a technician from the community, I simply had my father look it over. I know for a fact that he has saved the federal taxpayers millions of dollars because of his Purdue University training.

There is a natural rivalry between the technically oriented Purdue and the more liberal arts leaning IU. This rivalry is played out each year at the Oaken Bucket game. Since 1925, IU and Purdue have battled it out on the gridiron each November for the possession of an oaken bucket. An oaken bucket? Only people afflicted with Hoosieritis would fight over a bucket made of wood. If the prize were a golden trophy, a bronze figure carrying a football, or even a sacred stone, that would make more sense. Nope, an oaken bucket. Let's face it, Hoosiers are practical people. A bucket is much more useful than a trophy or statue. When the black and gold adorned team from West Lafayette wins the game, they probably take the bucket back to their classrooms for the year and use it in scientific experiments. I'll bet they have contests to see who can determine within a milliliter how much fluid the oaken bucket holds. If the cream and crimson wins the game, the oaken bucket is probably put on display for IU art students to sketch with a grand prize given to the best interpretation of the bucket's aesthetic significance. There is no sense wasting a perfectly good oaken bucket on a gladiator sport, now is there?

Hoosier Energy Solutions

"Or my name isn't Orville Redenbacher!" The Brazil, Indiana native, known for his exceptionally puffy popcorn, may have discovered the answer to the world's energy challenges. You'll recall his television commercials from the 1970's where he placed four ounces of his gourmet popcorn into a popper, and the exact same amount of ordinary popcorn into another popper. Suddenly, fluffy pieces of his popcorn overflowed from his popper, whereas the other popcorn could barely make it to the top. How did he do it? Could it be that Hoosier corn was exponentially more potent than corn from say, Nebraska?

Corn is one of the reasons that driving across Indiana can be quite tiresome. No, let's be honest and call it downright boring. During the growing season, drivers traversing the Hoosier State can be lulled into a mild coma simply by gazing at the view out the window. From the waters of the mighty Ohio River, to the surf along Lake Michigan's shore, all you will see is an unending sea of Orville's blessed corn plants, interrupted by the occasional stand of scrubby woods. If it's not corn, it's soybeans, followed by corn, then soybeans, then both, with one field of each on either side of the road. Hey, welcome to Indiana! Indiana is one of the largest producers of corn and soybeans in the country. And like its neighbors, Illinois and Ohio, Indiana is essentially a two-crop state. It's not that other crops won't grow in Indiana, it's just that Hoosier farmers, for the most part, choose to exclusively grow corn and soybeans. Everything else Indiana grows pales in comparison to these two kings of the Hoosier agricultural landscape.

Interestingly, these are two plants we choose not to grow in our Hoosier home garden. Soybeans are a no-brainer. What can you really do with soybeans once you've harvested them? Make your own tofu? Roast them in your oven like they are peanuts? Maybe, but not likely. We grew soybeans once. Once was enough. Corn is another matter. Many Hoosiers grow their own corn, and I know it's pretty good corn. I've bought many a bag of it at local roadside stands. We grew corn for a couple of years, but stopped when we discovered that we were merely being manipulated by the local Hoosier raccoon mafia. Call it the Great Raccoon Corn Conspiracy. How raccoons know exactly when to pick perfectly ripened corn is still a mystery to me. So, we gave up growing either of these plants in our garden. There's no sense in adding anymore to the monotony of Indiana's countryside.

But, perhaps Indiana's fields of corn and soybeans aren't so bad after all when we consider these simple facts: (1) There is a finite amount of crude oil in the world. Only a limited amount of ancient algae and zooplankton were created so that one day in the future we could drive our cars and SUV's to the mall. (2) The demand for crude oil increases daily. Why? Come on! There are more drivers born every day. The current population of the world is six billion, and they all want to drive their own cars. (3) There has yet to be invented an economically feasible alternative to the internal combustion engine and its thirst for crude oil products. Although psychologically influenced market fluctuations in the price of crude oil occasionally cause the price of refined petroleum based fuels to drop, the long-term trend is for the price to increase. It's simple economics. What's a solution for the present worldwide energy predicament?

Indiana to the rescue! Imagine all those miles of dull and boring corn and soybean fields transformed into the very fuel that is powering our driving trips across Hoosierland and elsewhere. No longer will we look upon these fields of deep green colored bean plants and golden brown tassels of corn with disdain. We'll see them as if they were gigantic oil wells pumping barrel upon barrel of black gold from the bowels of the earth. As an added bonus, we'll all have that warm fuzzy feeling that it's happening without harm to the planet or to any subterranean creatures that might inhabit the oil fields of the world. Imagine, no *Exxon Valdez* oil spills, no pipeline bursts, and no ugly oil derricks or refineries peppering the landscape (except in Lake County).

We're talking environmentally friendly fuel here – Ethanol (known by our neighbors to the south as White Lightnin' or Moonshine), and Soy or Bio Diesel. When we gaze upon these fields of green we will no longer wonder when will they ever end. Instead we'll know that Hoosier jobs in the farming and fertilizer sectors are being created to propel this alternative fuel effort forward. And, jobs are always good for the state's economy. We'll have the satisfaction of knowing that Indiana is doing its part to reduce the balance of payments between the USA and OPEC nations. It's a total win-win situation.

Until hydrogen powered fuel cells are perfected and made commercially viable… until batteries in electric and hybrid cars can be made significantly smaller and cheaper…until mass transit is available to all Americans…until hell freezes…you get the idea. As long as there are cars, trucks, SUV's, buses, trains, airplanes, lawnmowers, and chainsaws, we'll need the fuel to run them.

The future will be different. Count on it, but it won't be the energy horror the pundits of doom and gloom have forecast. Instead, there will be no gas lines, fuel rationing, or price gouging because E85 and Bio-diesel fuel will be available at every Hoosier gas station and beyond. With the demand for corn and soybeans rocketing in response to the pressure to make fuel, gardeners across Hoosierland will begin planting these crops in earnest.* You'll see new fields sprouting from fallow ground. In urban neighborhoods corn will rise from lots where abandoned houses once stood. Derelict factories will be replaced with soybean fields. Where there were once lawns of grass in front of businesses, schools, and churches there will soon stand fields of these holy and sacred crops. There won't be a square yard of tillable land in Indiana left untouched by the alternative fuel machine. If not corn and soybeans, then switchgrass. If you thought Indiana looked a little monochrome before, then hold on to your seats because "you ain't seen nuthin' yet!" Indiana will become a solid carpet of green. Heck, I might even plant some corn again in our home garden. Let us behold this vision of Hoosier leadership up to the world. Who knows, maybe even Illinois and Ohio might catch Hoosieritis, "or my name isn't Orville Redenbacher!"

*And to add to the world's food supply.

Hoosier State Tree

If someone was plucked out of their own neck-of-the-woods, dropped into the Hoosier State, and asked the question, "What is the State Tree of Indiana?" I seriously doubt they would answer correctly. I question whether most Hoosiers would even know the answer. Trivia buffs and arborists would respond with *Liriodendron tulipifera,* otherwise known as the Tulip tree, or Tulip Poplar. The Tulip tree is not a true poplar, but a member of the magnolia family. In the late spring this stately deciduous tree produces flowers that rival its southern magnolia cousin in beauty and fragrance.

You would think that every front yard in Indiana would sport one, or there would be one in the backyard to create a shady spot for children to play, but that would make way too much sense. The truth of the matter is that the Tulip tree is actually a rather uncommon tree in Indiana. Oh, you'll see the occasional one planted by some smart Hoosier, who looked up the Indiana State Tree on the internet, and thought it would be patriotic to plant one in their yard. However, you'll be hard pressed to find even one in most Hoosier neighborhoods.

The Tulip tree, although native to much of the Hoosier State, grows best not in Indiana but in the mountains of eastern Kentucky and Tennessee where it can reach heights of nearly two hundred feet! Like the coast redwood tree in California, which is the tallest tree in the western United States (and the world), the Tulip tree holds that honor in the eastern United States.* It is the Kentucky State Tree** (and Tennessee), and for obvious reasons – it grows all over the Bluegrass State. But, why, may we ask, is it the Indiana State tree? Why not pick a tree that's more uniquely Hoosier, one that you actually see growing everywhere in

Indiana? I've tried to grow them where I live, but every one I've planted eventually died.

Back to our question about a non-Hoosier being beamed into Indiana and asked to name the State Tree. After touring the cities, suburbs, and rural areas of the state I believe s/he would come to the conclusion that the Indiana State Tree is definitely not the *Liriodendron tulipifera,* but rather the *Picea pungens,* popularly known as the Colorado Blue Spruce.

You see, one of the ways Hoosieritis has impacted the brains of Indiana residents is their propensity to plant Colorado Blue Spruces in their yards. Hoosiers all seem to have been smitten with the Blue Spruce bug. There's no other plausible explanation for the plethora of these trees that can be found in almost every Hoosier's yard. Drive down any street in Indiana, and I mean any street, and you'll see a *Picea pungens* next to nearly every house. If not prominently displayed in the front yard, then you'll find one squirreled around the back. It is the king of trees in Indiana. Blue Spruces come in all shapes and sizes, from dwarf, shrub-like plants, to tall, conical specimens. Often you just find a lone Blue Spruce, but every now and then you'll come across whole hedges of them, lined up like soldiers defending the fort.

You might even make a game of identifying Blue Spruces. When you're out driving around and you see one point at it and say out loud "Blue Spruce!" Pretty soon you'll be yelling this phrase ad infinitum. Everyone else in the car will be ready to throw you out because of the frequency of your Blue Spruce sightings. Not only will you discover Blue Spruces in residential neighborhoods, but in front of businesses, schools, parks, government buildings, and out in the middle of cornfields as well.

On a routine drive around the northern loop of I-465 in Indianapolis you'll notice that Blue Spruces adorn the landscaping of all three freeway colleges, the University of

Phoenix, Indiana Weslyan University, and ITT Tech. Yes, each one of these institutions of higher education has Blue Spruces growing on the small lawns between the parking lots and their office building style classrooms. God help the schools that don't have at least one Blue Spruce planted in their schoolyard. Such an oversight would certainly be a violation of the "Hoosier State Tree Act" which clearly declares to every Hoosier property owner: "Thou shalt have a minimum of one *Picea pungens* growing on thy property or face the consequences." Face the consequences? That would be the ridicule of every other law abiding Hoosier for not complying with the statute. Once the infraction was detected, enforcement officials from the Indiana Department of Natural Resources would soon arrive at the non-complying property with Blue Spruce seedlings in hand ready to plant. The law is the law, and ignorance of that law is no excuse for disregarding it. All Hoosiers are hereby warned!

You may wonder why there are so many Blue Spruce trees growing in the Hoosier State. The answer is quite simple. The Arbor Society. It's their fault. Every year thousands of people receive invitations to join the National Arbor Society. For a mere fifteen dollars anyone can instantly become a member and a promoter of the earth's environmental health. As a way of saying thank you for supporting their cause the Arbor Society mails ten Blue Spruce seedlings to each new member with a note saying that these wonderful trees were especially selected to grow in your area. Seedlings grow into trees. Presto! Hoosier neighborhoods have become Blue Spruce plantations.

What other reasons do Hoosiers have for planting so many Blue Spruce trees? The answer lies in the very name of the tree. Blue! What color is nearly every other tree? Green. Pines are green, oaks are green, elms are green, and all other spruces are green. Tulip trees are green. There are, of course, red maple trees, and some reddish leaf crabapple trees. Yet, the numbers of these trees found in Hoosier landscaping is infinitesimal when compared with the mass proliferation of Blue Spruces.

Let's face it, trees aren't supposed to be blue. Hoosiers do plant other trees in their front yards, backyards, schoolyards, farms, and commercial properties. Norway Spruces are popular plantings, but they are native to Europe, and can get large and unwieldy. We often see Eastern White Pines, but that's the Michigan State Tree. Oaks are very common in Indiana, but the White Oak is the Illinois State tree. Forget the Buckeye. They're all nice trees, but the Blue Spruces simply stand out. After all, they're...blue. We Hoosiers love planting these unusually clad trees because they're kind of strange looking. Garden centers and tree nurseries throughout Indiana abound in potted Blue Spruces just waiting to be thrust into Hoosier soil. However, because of the success of the Blue Spruce plantings they are no longer uncommon trees in Indiana. They have become normal, or dare we say, native?

What is most interesting about the Colorado Blue Spruce, and its rapid propagation across Hoosierland, is the simple fact that the tree is <u>NOT</u> native to Indiana. Take a look at the name? Do you notice something peculiar about it? Does the word, Colorado, tip you off? The *Picea pungens* is native to Colorado and the rest of the Rocky Mountain states. It is the State Tree of both Colorado and Utah.

If Hoosiers had wanted to pick a State Tree that is a native evergreen, one that grows naturally in every one of Indiana's ninety-two counties, the *Juniperus virginiana,* or Eastern Redcedar, would be the logical choice. Redcedars are so tough they practically grow out of concrete, although they're partial to limestone infested soils. However, most Hoosiers consider the Redcedar a garbage tree, only suitable for making fence posts chests, closets, and bonfires. I like to think of it as the Indiana Redwood. My writer's studio sits atop seven Redcedar posts. The center portion of a Redcedar is the deepest red you'll ever see and has that uniquely unmistakable scent. Its wood is redder than the previously mentioned California redwood. They don't make chests out of *Sequoia sempervirens*, do they? Unfortunately, you don't see many Redcedars planted in front of Hoosier homes. Why? Because it isn't blue. It's green, just like every other tree. The verdict is in – the Blue Spruce has won the hearts of Hoosiers, and is a glaring symptom of the Hoosieritis disease.

Therefore, let us suggest that the Colorado Blue Spruce become the Hoosier State Tree. This proposal is not in any way to be confused with the already established Indiana State Tree, which can remain the Tulip tree. However, for the "unofficial" Hoosier State Tree, the tree that Hoosiers have obviously chosen with their green thumbs (or are they blue?), let us embrace the *Picea pungens.* And please, let's not tell Colorado or Utah anything about it. Imagine every Hoosier school kid planting dozens of them on Arbor Day. We can keep Hoosier landscaping the way Mother Nature intended it to look, blue! Care to guess where my Blue Spruce is in my yard? It's right out front.

*The Eastern White Pine *(Pinus strobus),* the state tree of Maine and Michigan, and the Eastern Hemlock (*Tsuga canadensis),* State Tree of Pennsylvania, have also been known to reach heights of nearly 200 feet.

**The Kentucky State Tree, like the Indiana State Tree, is the Tulip tree, but Indiana actually beat Kentucky to the punch by adopting the tree in 1931. In fact, the Great Seal of Indiana has four Tulip tree leaves on the lower part of its outer edges. The official flower of Indiana from 1923-31 was the Tulip tree's bloom, until the zinnia and later the peony took the honors. Kentucky, on the other hand, has had difficulty deciding on a State Tree. In 1956 the Commonwealth adopted the Tulip tree, but years later in 1973 it was discovered that an error had been made in recording the action of the state legislature. A huge uproar ensued with proponents of the Tulip tree and the Kentucky Coffee tree battling it out for the title. The Kentucky Coffee tree replaced the Tulip tree as the Kentucky State Tree in 1976, only to be overturned in 1994 with the reinstatement of the Tulip tree. It makes you wonder what they're drinking down there in Kentucky that they can't make up their minds about something as simple as a State Tree!

Hoosier National Park

Nestled on the very southern shore of Lake Michigan is Indiana's only national park, the Indiana Dunes National Lakeshore. Established in 1966 and operated by the National Park Service, this park, strewn in pieces along both sides of US 12 extends from US Steel in Gary to the far western edge of Michigan City. With its close proximity to Illinois, Michigan and Wisconsin, we might even call it, the Midwest's National Park.

Other Midwestern states might contest this claim. Take for instance Isle Royale National Park, located in Lake Superior approximately fifty miles off the northern tip of Michigan's Upper Peninsula, and twenty-five miles east of Grand Portage, Minnesota. Michiganders (it's in Michigan) could make a case that this is the Midwest's National Park given its pristine natural condition far away from the pollution of the industrial world. However, let's take a look at the map for a moment. Isle Royale National Park is an island in the middle of a very large lake, inaccessible by motor vehicle. To get there you have to take a boat or perhaps a helicopter. Furthermore, one could suggest that Isle Royale National Park shouldn't even be a United States Park, but a Canadian one since the park is actually closer to the Canadian shore. Maybe Isle Royale isn't a good candidate for the Midwest's National Park.

Travel west from Isle Royale National Park about two hundred miles and you'll arrive at another contender for the title of Midwest's National Park. Beginning on the west near International Falls, Minnesota, Voyageurs National Park is a combination of lakes and boreal forest stretching for over fifty miles southeast along the Canadian border making it almost as watery as Isle Royale. Of course, the big advantage of Voyageurs over Isle Royale is that you can actually drive to the park. Head due north from Minneapolis-St. Paul for three hundred miles and you'll arrive at the shore of Lake Kabetogama, one of the largest lakes within the park. However, if you were to visit Isle Royale first, then drive to Voyageurs, the recommended route from Grand Portage, Minnesota would be on Ontario Provincial Highway 11 through International Falls. Once you're at the park, the best way to see it is by boat, canoe, or kayak – hence, as with Isle Royale, a second vehicle is required. Naturally, boat rentals abound at the park. However, given the international border that provides the northern boundary of Voyageurs National Park, a case could be made for it also being managed within the scope of the Canadian National Park Service.

Isle Royale and Voyageurs National Parks are just too far from the geographic and population centers of the Midwest for either of them to be called the Midwest's National Park. Ah, but what about the Cuyahoga National Park in Ohio? Not only is this national park nowhere near Canada (over sixty miles as a crow flies), it's very easy to get to, since it practically borders the city of Cleveland on the north, and Akron on the south. Originally established as a National Recreation Area in 1974, it was redesignated a national park in 2000, making it one of the youngest national parks. What makes it different than Isle Royale and Voyageurs is that you can actually drive yourself to the park and enjoy its sights without having to bring or rent any other vehicles. And, it's close, very close, especially if you live in northern Ohio. Following the Cuyahoga River, the park offers pastoral views, forested hills, and a piece of the fabled Erie Canal. Yet, one interesting and potentially disturbing feature about Cuyahoga National Park is that part of it is built on an automobile junkyard. Do the words "junkyard" and "national park" seem a bit incongruous to you? Should this park be called the Midwest's National Park? Not in my mind, but I've got a bad case of Hoosieritis.

Let us return to the aforementioned Indiana Dunes National Lakeshore. Situated in the very heart of the Midwest with freeway access from almost every direction, and adjacent to the Midwest's largest city, Indiana Dunes is hands down the Midwest's National Park. Indiana Dunes National Lakeshore, or Hoosier National Park, has everything a national park could offer, from its sandy beaches and dunes, wildflowers, forests, swamps, hiking trails, campsites, historic homes, a working farm, and a very large, ocean-like lake. No other national park offers such diversity. Another interesting feature of the park is that its administrative headquarters was not built on a junkyard, but on the remains of a Nike missile base. Can you think of a better use for this Cold War era relic than for it to be transformed into a place of beauty, peace, and outdoor enjoyment for all?

I remember as a young child going by the base on the way to my Great Uncle Carl's farm and admiring the sample of the heavily finned missile that stood in front of the complex. When you're a young boy, images of rockets and missiles stick in your consciousness. When I grew up a little, I built model rockets much like the one I saw displayed on the base. Now I just buy bottle rockets from my local Hoosier fireworks store. My uncle's farm must have been of national strategic value to have had an ABM battery next to it. Apparently the missile base's septic system was important, for it was located on the north side of his farm. Now, my uncle is long gone, but his farm continues to flourish since it was purchased by the park service in 1972. In fact, his farm never looked better than it does today.

The Chellberg Farm, as it's called, is a vintage turn of the 20th century working farm within the Indiana Dunes National Lakeshore. My Swedish ancestors founded the farm in the 1860's along Mineral Springs Road where my paternal grandmother, Naomi Victoria Chellberg, was born along with her older sister, Ruth, and her younger brother, Carl, who ran the farm until it was sold to the park service. My early childhood memories consist of Swedish Christmas parties in the old red brick farmhouse, and seeing my uncle's sheep that he kept in a pen back by the edge of the woods. I remember one Christmas receiving one of those black plastic "8" balls, that when you flipped it upside down, would pop up answers to life's deepest questions. Sometimes I wish I still had it.

Visitors to my Uncle Carl's farm can sample a taste of what it was like to live on the land the old fashioned way, something that few of us in our modern supermarket world actually experience. Each spring people flock to the Chellberg Farm and the neighboring Bailly Homestead for the Maple Sugar Time Festival where hundreds of poor, unsuspecting *Acer saccharum* are tapped for their sugar rich sap. In the fall, the focus shifts back to the farm for the Duneland Harvest Festival. Considering what farming means to Indiana, touring the Chellberg Farm is the ultimate Hoosieritis experience.

The crowning glory of the Midwest's National Park is its highest point. On the far northeastern edge of the park towering a colossal 126 feet above the shore of Lake Michigan stands Mount Baldy. By Colorado standards (I mention the Rocky Mountain State since we Hoosiers love their State Tree so much – see the chapter, *Hoosier State Tree*) Mount Baldy doesn't seem like much of a mountain, but when one is afflicted with Hoosieritis, it appears to be a lofty peak. Actually, Mount Baldy is not a mountain but a giant sand dune. Be careful scaling its heights as climbers will quickly discover an abundance of sand in their shoes.

Hoosier Standard Time

"Does Anybody Really Know What Time It Is?" This isn't merely the hit song by the rock group, Chicago, it's a serious question for anyone living in or visiting the Hoosier State. Does anybody really know what time it is...in Indiana? The answer isn't always as simple as looking at your watch. For those of you not from Indiana (or states that border Indiana) this whole discussion may seem irrelevant or nonsensical, but knowing what time it is Indiana is often a necessity for anyone doing business in the state. Why? Because not every place in Indiana is on the same time! Maybe that's why Robert Lamm wrote the song. He was from Chicago, and probably wasn't really sure what time it was in Indiana.

Hoosiers like going it alone, bucking the trends. That's the nature of Hoosieritis. Up until 2006, Arizona, Hawaii, and Indiana did not observe Daylight Savings Time. This anomaly created some chronometrical challenges in figuring out the time in these states. Is the time in Hawaii five or six hours earlier than in the Eastern Time Zone? If I'm in California and drive to Arizona will the time at my destination be one hour later, or the same time? However, unlike the two western states, Indiana complicates the question because some of its counties are on Eastern and others on Central Time.

It's not unheard of to partition states into two different time zones. Just to the south of the Hoosier State are the longitudinally endowed states of Kentucky and Tennessee, both of which divide their territories into Eastern and Central Time zone sections. Yet, Indiana would not be described as a very wide state from east to west as these states clearly are. Dividing the Hoosier State with different times seems quite unnecessary, perhaps even a little nutty.

Why the two time zones, you ask? The answer is simple: Hoosieritis.

Yes, Hoosieritis strikes again! When the Hoosier State was on Standard Time all year, what made telling the time worse was the counties bordering major cities in neighboring states, which followed Daylight Savings Time, would set their clocks in sync with those cities. If you lived in Jeffersonville, right across the Ohio River from Louisville, Kentucky, you followed Louisville time. Just up the river in Dearborn and Ohio counties, adjacent to Cincinnati, you set your clocks according to the Queen City. Shoot on up north to the counties that ring the southern shore of Lake Michigan, these were on Chicago time. Evansville and the counties in the southwest corner of the state followed the time in Illinois and western Kentucky. For all practical purposes these areas of the Hoosier State were illegally on Daylight Savings Time, unless of course you had school children. For some reason, and the most likely explanation probably had to do with the scheduling of high school sporting events, the schools in these counties did not follow Daylight Savings Time, but set their clocks on what we might call Hoosier Standard Time, or HST.

For several years our family, residents of Dearborn County, had two clocks in our home, one on Cincinnati time, called fast time, and another for the schools, or slow time. You had to pay careful attention to which clock you were viewing as to which time you desired to know. The VCR in the family room was set on fast time because all of our local TV stations were in Ohio. The alarm clock in our bedroom showed slow time, to coordinate with the kid's school. Since I worked in Cincinnati, my wristwatch was set on fast time, and my wife, who worked as a substitute teacher for the school system, set hers on slow time. This worked pretty well until one day we discovered that this distinction of time only applied to schools, and not the rest of the local government institutions. My wife was called to jury duty and showed up an hour late because she assumed the courts would be on slow time, the official time of Indiana, just like the schools. Wrong! The Dearborn County courthouse was on fast time. Thankfully the sheriff did not issue a bench warrant for her tardiness.

Events in our community always mentioned whether they were being held on fast or slow time, just to make sure folks showed up at the correct time. During the dark months, all of the clocks were on the same time, which made life a bit easier until Cincinnati sprang forward each spring. It was possible that during Daylight Savings Time some parts of Indiana were on Eastern Daylight Time, Eastern Standard Time, and Central Daylight Time. Figure that out, would you? For example, let's say the time at our home in Bright was 9:00 (EDT). At that same moment the time in Indianapolis it would be 8:00 (EST). In Gary it would be 8:00 (CDT).

For obvious reasons, these time variations created havoc for people in business, and those traveling through the Hoosier State. Although we live only twenty-two miles from the Cincinnati-Northern Kentucky Airport, we'd frequently fly out of the Indianapolis Airport about a hundred miles away to save money on airfare. We'd always have to ask ourselves first, is Indianapolis on our time or not? When does our flight take off? Sometimes flights from Indianapolis would be routed through Cincinnati. For example, a 10:00 flight from Indianapolis would land in Cincinnati at 11:50, even though the length of the flight was barely an hour. Similarly, a flight to Chicago, another sub-hour flight, would arrive in the Windy City at about 11:00, unless it was during Standard time, which would make it 10:00. Confused by all of this chronological mumbo-jumbo? It made perfect sense to us Hoosiers, but then we're the ones with the contagious disease known as Hoosieritis.

On April 28, 2005, the confusion around "Hoosier Standard Time" came to a screeching halt, or so it appeared. At 11:36 p.m., the Indiana House, in a 51-46 vote, passed Senate Bill 127 mandating Daylight Savings Time for all of Indiana's ninety-two counties beginning in April 2006. After a forty-year hiatus, the Hoosier State was rejoining the other forty-seven DST states in springing forward and falling back every year. Hurray! No more fast and slow time for our home clocks. Arizona and Hawaii could continue to hold the banner of non-conforming Standard Time states.

The new Governor of Indiana, Mitch Daniels, had fulfilled a campaign promise he made during his gubernatorial run, that of getting Hoosiers on the same time, or had he? Perhaps he had only partially succeeded. Look at the vote to change to Daylight Savings Time, 51-46, the bare minimum for passing the bill. The senate had passed it a day earlier in a 28-22 vote. Neither vote was exactly what you would call a huge mandate for change. The debate over this bill was, shall we say, emotionally charged and filled with arm-twisting persuasion of the highest order, ending in a nearly midnight decision. I'm sure that some of the legislators just wanted to go home to bed and voted for the bill out of their need to avoid sleep deprivation.

Governor Daniels was thwarted in his quest to unite Hoosiers in a single standardized time. Ten defiant western counties insisted that they remain on Central rather than join the rest of Indiana on Eastern Time. Now, when it's 9:00 in Indianapolis it's still 8:00 in Gary or Evansville. The disease of Hoosieritis prevented a strong consensus in the pursuit to achieve Hoosier Standard Time, a vision that will remain only a possibility for the future.

You can easily find out what time it is in Indiana if you have Internet access. Just log on to: "What Time is it in Indiana" and you will be guided to a website sponsored by the Monroe County School Corporation in Bloomington,

Indiana. Since 1997, this website has helped people figure out the answer to this age-old question: What time is it in Indiana? Perhaps Hoosier Standard Time isn't so much about uniformity anyway, but simply about acknowledging the time in whatever part of the state you happen to be in at the moment.

Not Really Hoosier

In the movie version of Meredith Wilson's classic musical, *The Music Man*, little Ronnie Howard sang a song that once you've heard it, you can never get out of your head! That song: "Gary Indiana." Or is it? Is Gary really in Indiana? Is Hammond? Is Crown Point? Is the place of my birth, East Chicago? Ah, with that last question, maybe we're getting somewhere.

My family's roots are strong in the northwest corner of Indiana. My maternal great-grandfather, Frank Martin, was mayor of Hammond. During that same period of time, my paternal great-uncle, Hugh Studebaker, was an alderman in Hammond. My distant cousin, William A. Wirt, was an educator in Gary back in the early 20th century. My grandfather, Alden K. "Studie" Studebaker, was the contractor who built most of the early homes in the town of Dune Acres (a town founded by cousin William Wirt). My German great-grandmother Dietrich ran a grocery store in downtown Hammond. When my Swedish ancestors came to America in the 1860's they became farmers in Porter. My father and uncle were born and raised in Dune Acres, and my mother was from Hammond. Okay, I'll shut up about my family's connections to the Calumet Region. But, it does beg the question, when I consider my Hoosier lineage, "Am I really a Hoosier?"

The Calumet Region, or more simply, "The Region" or "Da Region," as it's often called, is a unique place in Indiana. Inasmuch as Chicago is not really like the rest of Illinois, the Calumet Region really isn't Indiana. When you look at the culture, media, industry, mentality, and what time it is, this little corner of Indiana can easily be considered a part of the State of Chicago. I can't prove it, but would venture to say that this proposed city-state of

Chicago is economically more dominant than the rest of Indiana and Illinois combined. Heck, throw Wisconsin in there too! All of The Region's highways and railroads lead to Chicago. The Gary airport isn't just called the Gary Regional Airport; rather it's called the Gary/Chicago Regional Airport. All of the signs pointing north along I-65 from Indianapolis do not indicate Gary as the final terminus, but Chicago. I-65 doesn't even go to Chicago, but the sign says it does.

Another way Hoosieritis does not show up in the Calumet Region is in its sports allegiances. No self-respecting resident of The Region would ever admit to being a Colts or Pacers fan. No way! We can see this allegiance played out in the 2007 Super Bowl where The Region was firmly on the side of the Chicago Bears. No doubt there was great gnashing of teeth and wearing of sackcloth and ashes following *da Bears* 29-17 loss to the Colts.

Another very non-Hoosier aspect of the Calumet Region is its harbors. When one thinks of Indiana the words "harbor" or "port city" rarely come to mind.   Grain elevators, yes, harbors, no. There are harbors on the Indiana side of the Ohio River at Jeffersonville (near Louisville, Kentucky) and Mount Vernon (near Evansville), but these harbors only accommodate barge traffic. When we say harbor, we're referring to deep draft ocean-going ships. Head straight north from the Ohio River to the Calumet Region and you'll discover Indiana Harbor in East Chicago, and the Port of Indiana (officially the Burns Waterway Harbor) near Portage. Thanks to the St. Lawrence Seaway, Indiana (and other Great Lakes states) has a harbor with direct access to the world's oceans.

While we're on the subject of water, let's consider Indiana's contribution to the world of surfing. Surfing in Indiana, you ask? That's not very Hoosier, is it? While the California cities of Huntington Beach and Santa Cruz battle it out in court for the title, "Surf City, USA," the designation should rightly go to one of the Calumet Region's municipalities. But, which one? The waves break with great form all along Indiana's 45-mile shoreline, from Michigan City to Whiting Beach. Whiting Beach…now that has a nice ring to it!

Encompassing just over three square miles along the shore of Lake Michigan, and bordering its larger neighbor, Hammond, Whiting with its municipal beachfront park and Whihala County Park tops my list as the best candidate for Surf City, USA. Better known for one of the largest oil refineries in the country (Amoco, now BP, where my grandfather, great-uncle, father, and uncle once worked), and its annual Pierogi Festival, Whiting is the ideal Hoosier, dare we say, American surfing spot. Besides, how many places in the world can you surf with a clear view of oil refineries, steel mills, and electric power plants? Can Huntington Beach or Santa Cruz offer this unique industrial surfing experience? Hardly! Besides, the effluent coming out of the refinery warms the waters around Whiting just when the waves are at their peak, fall and winter.

Huntington Beach is very nice, it really is. I used to go there with my wife and daughter when we lived in LA. Back in the 1970's I lived in Santa Cruz while attending the University of California, and used to run along its beaches for exercise and fresh sea air. But, neither of these California surfing locations holds a candle to Whiting, or should we say, flare stack? Whiting Beach also has a tremendous advantage over these beaches, or any other beach in California or Hawaii. No shark attacks.* I rest my case. Whiting is Surf City, USA, easily accessible by Americans on all three coasts, East, West, and Midwest. Bring it on Huntington Beach and Santa Cruz! If you're reading this Brian Wilson or Jan & Dean, there's a potential song that could be written about Whiting Beach. Hey, the surf is definitely up in Indiana!

While we're on the subject of heavy industry, what distinguishes the Calumet Region from much of Indiana is its foul, rotten smell. Residents of Northwest Indiana are so immersed in the air around their homes that they simply don't notice the stench. It really stinks there, even at the beach. For instance, if you're traveling into The Region on your way to Chicago, via the Indiana Toll Road or Interstate 80/94, you will immediately notice that something smells funny. Where does the smell originate, you ask? Take a look to your right and you will see the culprit. Lined along the western portion of Indiana's lakeshore are an array of steel mills, oil refineries, and chemical plants. These give the Calumet Region the distinction of being the armpit of Indiana, and you know how bad armpits smell. I can say this because I was born there!

The now defunct Union Carbide plant in Whiting used to churn out such foul smelling odors that, according to my father it, "would make me want to throw up." My mother, who grew up in the Roberstdale section of Hammond would always talk about the soot covered snow that would cover the yard in winter. She grew up thinking that snow was more black than white! On the morning of August 27, 1955 the nearby Standard Oil refinery in Whiting (now BP) literally blew up, launching tons of metal shrapnel into the surrounding neighborhood. The fire burned for several days until it consumed fifty-nine storage tanks of fuel. My father had been working on the suspect hydroformer just hours before it exploded. My siblings and I are eternally grateful that both of our parents escaped the ensuing carnage.

The fetid smells of industry continue to pour from Gary's and Burns Harbor's steel mills. Even with Lake Michigan nearby, there's hardly a clean drop of water to be found. Do the words, mercury, nitrogen oxides, sulfur oxides, hydrocarbons, carbon monoxide, aerosols, asbestos, chlorofluorocarbons (CFCs), ground level ozone, hazardous air pollutants (HAPs), hydrochlorofluorocarbons (HCFCs), methane, particulate patter (PM), propellants, radon, refrigerants, substitutes, and volatile organic compounds (VOCs) ring a bell?** That's not very Hoosieritis at all. Hoosieritis is about vast open corn and soybean field of green, forested hills, and lazy fishing days along babbling brooks. Let's face it, the air and water pollution are so rampant that the entire Calumet Region should be declared a national Superfund site! A word to the wise: Do not eat fish from Wolf Lake or the Little Calumet River. I'm just warning you.

And, as strange as it may seem, a very un-Hoosieritis like event took place in Gary in 2001 and 2002. No, it wasn't a steelworkers convention, but the hosting of the Miss USA Pageant. A beauty pageant in Gary, Indiana? Check it out for yourself if you don't believe me. During the first year none other than actor, William Shatner, of Star Trek-TJHooker-Boston Legal-Priceline.com fame, hosted the pageant. Even Martha Stewart was a judge that year. It was exciting to see these bikini-clad young ladies strolling along the beach with the US Steel mill in the background. Was it worth the millions Gary paid for this honor? No doubt the pageant put the City of Gary on the radar of every viewer who tuned in on those evenings. Certainly Donald Trump had a hand in Gary's selection as the pageant site. He owned a casino there, and he's not even a Hoosier.

And finally, running throughout the entire length of The Region is the very un-Hoosier-like transportation conveyance governed by the Northern Indiana Commuter Transportation District, otherwise known as the South Shore. The South Shore is one of the last remaining electric interurban railroads in the United States. Begun in the early

1900's, this rail line runs from downtown Chicago all the way to South Bend, a distance of nearly one hundred miles. At its peak during World War II the South Shore transported six million passengers a year. Today that amount has fallen to a little more than half that figure, but with gasoline prices sometimes surging over four dollars per gallon, that number is bound to rise. Plans are now in the works to create new trunk lines down to Lowell and Valparaiso. Perhaps this albatross of early 1900's technology is the new wave of eco-friendly transportation!

As a small child I remember my father riding the South Shore every day from the Dune Acres Station (now gone, use Dune Park) all the way to downtown Chicago. He'd leave the house at 6:20 a.m. and drive my maternal grandfather's black 1956 Buick to the station to catch the 6:40 train. My sister and I called it the "Rrroom-Rrroom Car" because of the noise the leaky exhaust system would make when you fired it up. My father worked for Amoco-Standard Oil in the old building on 910 South Michigan Avenue. He would get off at the Roosevelt Road Station and be in his office just after eight o'clock. A monthly ticket cost him about fifty bucks in the 1960's. Today it'll run you close to two hundred dollars, which is still a bargain when you consider the price of parking in downtown Chicago.

Once I was turning onto US 12 near Burns Harbor and spotted a South Shore train heading eastbound parallel to the highway. Hoosieritis immediately overpowered my right foot as I put the pedal to the metal in an effort to keep pace with the train. After a brief moment of glory when I pulled even with the train I gave up the pursuit when I noticed that my speedometer read 79 miles per hour! Bear in mind, Hoosieritis is a disease that compels one to not allow a commuter train, of all vehicles, to best one in a race down the highway, but then I saw no sense in giving the Indiana

State Police or the Porter County Sheriff a reason to pull me over. Hoosieritis has its practical side too.

As you can see, the Calumet Region is a unique corner of Indiana and requires special treatment in this book. Although it is technically in the State of Indiana, it's not really Hoosier. Thankfully there are scores of other Indiana counties beckoning you to discover this serious malady that afflicts the vast majority of Indiana residents.

*According to the October 10, 2006, Northwest Indiana Times article, *Whiting: Surf's up as lake's waves offer wild rides*: "Just east of Whiting Park last Wednesday, a contingent of surfers were negotiating (no exaggeration here) 7- to 10-foot waves. Perhaps the only thing that distinguished the scene from a beach in Hawaii were the petro-producing refineries rather than lava-spewing mountains in the background."

**List compiled by Allison Hannon, Senior Thesis entitled, *A New Northwest Indiana: A Cleaner Economy and Environment*, Environmental Studies Program, University of Chicago, May 20, 2005

<u>More Hoosieritis</u>

Hoosier Architecture

The disease of Hoosieritis extends from Indiana's residential architecture, to the objects Hoosiers place in front of their residences, to the way roads are labeled. Take the A-frame house, for instance. A-frame houses are a natural choice for people who live in mountainous regions where deep snows are common. The sharp angle of their gables shed these snows, preventing damage resulting from the excessive weight of accumulating snow on a more conventional roof. And, why do we find so many A-frame houses in Indiana? Survey a topographical map of Indiana and you'll discover that it's not exactly mountainous. The highest point in the Hoosier State is a grove of trees in Wayne County called Hoosier Hill – elevation: 1,257 feet above sea level. That's not what you would call a snow capped mountain worthy of an A-frame chalet, would you?

Weird architecture doesn't stop with A-frames. Berm houses are also popular. For those unfamiliar with the term, berm house, think "Little House on the Prairie," where the walls and roof are covered with dirt. For the Laura Ingalls Wilder family in the middle of the nineteenth century Great Plains where wood was scarce, a house made of earth was the only option. However, modern day Hoosiers have access to some of the most well stocked warehouse style lumberyards on the face of the planet. You know their names. Constructing berm style buildings is really not necessary, unless it's your life-long dream to live like a gopher.

One of my favorite berm houses can be seen heading south from Indianapolis on I-74 at around milepost 100 at the Marion-Shelby County line. Look to the west and you'll see it surrounded by trees with a cupola at the top. I've often wondered what inspired the builder to erect it. Another berm building is Sunman-Dearborn Middle School in St. Leon where each of our children has attended. It is said that berm buildings are well insulated by the earth around them and are natural shelters from tornadoes and storms. So, why didn't they build the high school next door the same way? Perhaps the "berm" bug didn't affect the entire school board. Maybe all of us Hoosiers should consider piling up earth around our houses. It would save energy, wouldn't it? Where's my shovel?

Hoosier Front Yards

It is not just the style of architecture that distinguishes many Hoosier homes, but the objects Hoosiers place in their front yards. Topping the list of front yard phenomena are rocks, and, not just any rocks, but gigantic boulders. I don't know what Hoosier quarry produced these enormous rocks. Usually when one thinks of Hoosier rock, it is the Bedford limestone of southern Indiana, a common building material. These front yard rocks are clearly not limestone, but granite possibly dragged into Indiana from out of state by the last glacial epoch. Why are these boulders sitting in Hoosier front yards? Is it to make it difficult for visitors to park? Is it to defend the home against terrorist attacks? Is it to keep up with the Jones' – a "my rock is bigger than your rock" scenario?

Next on the list of strange front yard objects are fake animals. I have a neighbor who has deer statues in his lawn, and every time I see them I want to slam on my brakes for fear that they'll run in front of my car. Several years ago I hit a deer less than a half-mile from our house. I had been dodging herds of them one November evening as I drove the hilly route home from Lawrenceburg. I thought I was home free as I rounded a curve on our road, when a half-dozen of them jumped out in front of my car. Collision was unavoidable. Thankfully the deer went under my car and did only minimal damage. Every time I do an oil change I can still see deer fur attached to the underside of the car. When it comes to deer hunting, I now like to say, "Who needs a gun when you have a car?" Now, you can understand my apprehension as I drive past the house with deer statuary.

The other popular animal statuary that can be found in Hoosier front yards are bears. Although I should be scared of bears given their fierce nature, I'm not as concerned about their possibly jumping out in front of my car as I am deer. Wild bears are pretty much extinct in Indiana, except for the zoo. I'd like to change out those deer up the road for a couple of bears, and I know just where to get them too. There are special stores that supply the Hoosier thirst for animal statues and other objects. Don't miss these stores: just north of Grissom Air Force Base on US 31, just south of Indianapolis on SR 37, or northbound from Louisville on I-65 at exit 5, and on I-74 just west of Batesville. Maybe there's a store near you.

There are many other front yard curiosities that are parked in front of Hoosier homes. In rural areas old tractors often adorn the landscaping. It's not uncommon to find Farmall, Allis-Chalmers, Fordson, John Deere, and other antique tractors lined up like used cars for sale. In many cases, they are for sale. Antique wagon wheels are popular Hoosier front yard fixtures. My uncle has an old manure spreader, but at least he has the decency to keep it sequestered behind high fences in his backyard. My absolute favorite front yard object is not far from the previously mentioned statue store on US 31. As you're heading north of Grissom Air Force Base about a mile or two up the road there is a front yard where you'll see the largest yellow rocking chair on planet Earth. If the Jolly Green Giant (now a resident of Greentown, see the chapter, *Hoosier Places*) were looking for a place to sit down after a long day working in the fields this would be the chair. Look for it during the warmer months.

Hoosier River

Any native born Hoosier reading the title of this heading will instinctively know the name of the Hoosier River. When I asked my Indiana native born father to name the Hoosier River, "Wabash," instantly rolled off his tongue. The native American tribe, Miami, called it Wah-Bah-Shik-Ka. The French attempted to pronounce this name, Ouabache, until English speakers rendered it in its current form. *A River Runs Through It* certainly describes the Wabash's path through the Hoosier State. Anyone driving in a latitudinal trek across the Indiana will unavoidably at some point cross the Wabash River. It is officially the State River of Indiana, and its influence on Hoosier culture inspired the official State Song, "On the Banks of the Wabash, Far Away."

There are other rivers that impact the Hoosier State. The Ohio River delineates the entire southern border of Indiana, dividing it from the Commonwealth of Kentucky. The White River meanders through Indianapolis on its way southwest to the Wabash River. A large dam on a branch of the Whitewater River is the backstop for the Brookville Reservoir, one of the largest lakes in the Hoosier State. The Kankakee River clips the northwest section of the state, dividing Indiana from its less Hoosier region (see the chapter, *Not Really Hoosier*). However, none of these waterways inspires Hoosiers like the Wabash. Once a part of the early 1800's canal system, it was replaced by the railroad that bears its name, the Wabash Cannonball. Yet, what is most interesting about the Wabash River is that its headwaters are not in Indiana, but in Ohio. Ohio! That just doesn't sound right, does it? After all, Ohio already has a river.

Hoosier Roads

Care to guess where the shortest state highway is in Indiana? It's State Route 520 located in northeast Porter County. At one-quarter of a mile long, SR 520 is the shortest highway in the state, and possibly in the entire country! That's no joke – it's a mere ¼ of a mile long. I measured it myself. This north-south diminutive stretch of asphalt connects US 12 and US 20 in the Town of Pines. Why is it a state highway? Was this a ploy by the Town of Pines to get state maintenance for one of their streets? After all, SR 520 has another name, Maple Street. SR 520 is home to a fire station, a motel, and other assorted buildings, and since it connects two major US highways together, it's the handiest little state highway in Indiana.

Speaking of roads, Hoosiers have given them some of the most creative names imaginable. I'm not speaking of city streets, but of rural roads. My cousin, who has a llama farm in northern Shelby Country, lives on Road W 1100 N. Logically, one could see the rationale in naming this road W 1100 N by observing that she lives in the northern part of the county, hence the "N" designation...and, the "1100" part would indicate a road that is eleven miles from the center of the county...and, the "W" means she lives west of the county center. However, hold on here a moment, what kind of road name is W 1100 N? Oh, I live on W 1100 N, come on by for a visit some time. Right! Depending on the county, you will find these numbered roads labeling many rural Hoosier thoroughfares. Thankfully my county, Dearborn, has the sense to give roads non-numbered names, like Bunkum, Sneakville, and Toddy. Those are names you can remember.

Do you think you can remember this name, the Illiana Expressway? Better get used to it. A proposal has been submitted to build a toll road connecting I-65 in Lake County with I-57 near Beecher, Illinois, making it the third east-west high-speed roadway in the Chicago-Lake County area. At least they're not naming it the "I-65-I-57 Connector." One thing that you can be sure of is that when the Illliana Expressway is opened for the first time, the fastest cars on it will bear Illinois license plates. Hoosiers know all too well that the fastest cars on their roads are from Illinois. I guess that's called, Illinoisitis.

Hoosier State Car

Of course, roads wouldn't exist it weren't for the vehicles that travel upon them. Indiana has produced some very notable ones, namely, the Auburn, Cord, Duesenberg, Marmon, Stutz, and Studebaker. Auburn cars were built in the town from which its name was derived. Auburn also produced the Cord, a front-wheel drive car with retractable headlights, very innovative for the 1930's. Many of the highly acclaimed hot-rod Duesenberg and Stutz cars were built at factories in Indianapolis. The Marmon was also an Indianapolis built car, and its Wasp model won the first Indy 500 race in 1911. This was the first car ever equipped with a rear-view mirror (hence, the driver, Ray Harroun, didn't need a co-pilot to ride along and warn him about other cars in the race).

However, the Godfather of all the Hoosier cars is the Studebaker, and should rightfully be called, the Hoosier State Car. This assessment, of course, has absolutely nothing to do with the fact that my last name is Studebaker, not at all. By sheer numbers, Studebaker out-built and out-sold every other Hoosier automobile manufacturer combined. From 1902-66, Studebakers sold in the millions, whereas the others sold in the thousands at best. Before Studebaker assembled cars, they built horse-drawn wagons and carriages, gazillions of them! Studebaker wagons were supplied to the Union Army during the Civil War, and carried many a pioneer westward to their fortune. It was Hoosier destiny that Studebaker would become one of the first American automobile companies.

Cords, Duesenbergs, Marmons, and Stutzs were cars for the rich, whereas Studebakers were for the average person. Back in its heyday, anybody could afford a Studebaker, at least a used one. They even out-sold Ford during the 1920's. Now, most people under the age of thirty don't have a clue what a Studebaker car is. I often cite the *The Muppet Movie* as a reference point for identification purposes. Fozzie the Bear drove Kermit the Frog and Miss Piggy to Hollywood in a multi-colored, bullet-nosed 1951 Studebaker Commander. The actual car is on display at the Studebaker National Museum in South Bend. Fozzie definitely had Hoosieritis, as evidenced by his saying, "Ahh, a bear in his natural habitat - a Studebaker."

Interestingly, during World War II, over 150,000 Studebaker US6 trucks were sent to the Soviet Union, and were dubbed, "Studers," by the Soviet troops. These durable, well-built trucks helped the war effort on the Eastern Front, and were sometimes used as platforms to launch rockets. Even Russians were exposed to the Hoosieritis contagion.

My dear uncle has a very serious case of Hoosieritis. He owns at least a half-dozen "Studies" in varying degrees of driving condition. Actually, only one of them runs, a '63 Cruiser. The rest of his Studebaker fleet is returning the raw materials from whence they were derived, back to Mother Earth, in the backyard of his residence (see above, *Hoosier*

Front Yards). I like to refer to his faded green Lark station wagon as the "Fred Flinstone Car," since the floorboards under the driver have rusted out and are open to foot propulsion. "Yabba, dabba, doo!"

My father has a '61 Champ pickup truck, formerly owned by the City of Los Angeles Department of Water and Power. I drove behind him for nearly a week while he towed this truck from California back to its native Indiana. Since the tailgate of the truck reads, "Studebaker," I knew which trailer to follow. After he passed in 2014, I sold it to a woman who grew up in Los Angeles driving her father's Champ pickup as a teenager – a perfect home for it. Some of my Studebaker relatives are also smitten with automotive Hoosieritis. My cousin, Julie Studebaker, owns a bright red '64 Avanti, her brother Paul has a white '63 Avanti (now in the family trust), and brother, Larry, has a '64 Champ.

Today, Japanese cars have moved into the automotive manufacturing landscape of the Hoosier State. For the past twenty years, Subaru of Indiana Automotive, Inc., also known as SIA, has been churning out cars at a plant just south of Lafayette. Since 1996, Toyota Motor Manufacturing Indiana, or TMMI, has built minivans, SUV's, and pickup trucks at a plant in Princeton thirty miles north of Evansville. Recently, Honda built a half-billion dollar plant near Greensburg to produce its popular Civic. Apparently these transplanted companies have got the "made in Indiana" Hoosieritis bug. If building cars in Indiana worked for the homegrown Studebaker, then maybe it will for them too.

Hoosieritis Photos*

The fireworks store where the book, *Hoosieritis,* got its birth. On the Fourth of July the parking lot is always packed with cars from Ohio. Location: On US 52 in West Harrison, Dearborn County. Chapter: *Hoosier Values.*

*All photos taken by the author and his son, Danny Studebaker, unless otherwise noted.

The coolest place in Indiana. A cutout of Indiana's "patron saint," James Dean, inviting you to enter and visit the shrine dedicated to his memory. Location: Fairmount Historical Museum, Fairmount, Grant County. Chapter: *Hoosier Identity*.

There really is a castle in Castleton! This White Castle, home of the "slider" steam-cooked hamburger, is one of fifty-seven restaurants in the Hoosier State. Location: 82nd Street near Allisonville Road, Indianapolis, Marion County. Chapter: *Hoosier Places.*

The finest example of Hoosieritis castle architecture. Note the rather prominent "Hoosier State Tree" on the left. These trees adorn the gardens surrounding many Indiana county courthouses. The tower clock accurately shows the "Hoosier Standard Time." Location: Rochester, Fulton County. Chapters: *Hoosier Places, Hoosier State Tree,* and *Hoosier Standard Time.*

One of Indiana's post-secondary educational institutions with its Colorado Blue Spruce or "Hoosier State Tree" framing its sign. Location: Indiana Wesleyan University, visible from I-465, Indianapolis, Marion County. Chapter: *Hoosier State Tree.*

Start your engines and fasten your seat belts! You are about to enter the real world Indy 500. Vrrrrrooommm! Location: Southwest junction of I-74 and I-465, Indianapolis, Marion County. Chapter: *Hoosier Capital.*

An idyllic picnic spot under a mighty oak tree where the author had lunch one lazy summer day, and the greenest spot in all of Greentown. Incidentally, the garbage can seen on the left is painted green. Way to go, Greentown – you know your true colors! Location: Just to the right on US 35 upon entering Greentown from the west, Howard County. Chapter: *Hoosier Places*.

The Hoosier State's primary agricultural products (corn and soybeans) growing peacefully side by side saving the world from its dependency on fossil fuels. Location: State Route 26 near Phlox, Howard County. Chapter: *Hoosier Energy Solutions.*

The Wabash River, the "Hoosier State River," as seen from Wabash....Ohio! The headwaters of the Wabash River are actually in the Buckeye State. What's wrong with this picture? Perhaps Indiana should annex Mercer County from Ohio to keep the river exclusively Hoosier. Location: Bridge on State Route 29 just east of Wabash, Mercer County, Ohio. Chapter: *More Hoosieritis.*

What would Indiana be without its farms? The Chellberg Farm, the ultimate Hoosieritis experience, established by my Swedish ancestors in the 1860's, and the birthplace of my grandmother. Location: Indiana Dunes National Lakeshore, Mineral Springs Road, Porter County. Chapter: *Hoosier National Park.*

The surf's up on Lake Michigan! Whiting Beach is the only beach in the United States to offer the industrial surfing experience. Notice the BP refinery in the background. Cowabunga! Location: Whiting, Lake County. Chapter: *Not Really Hoosier.*

The shortest state highway in Indiana (and possibly the United States). This photo shows nearly all of its entire ¼ mile length. Location: Indiana State Route 520, Town of Pines, Porter County. Chapter: *More Hoosieritis.*

The street sign near my cousin's llama farm. What imaginative names we Hoosiers use to label our roads! Location: Shelby County. Chapter: *More Hoosieritis.*

You pronounce this street name like a piece of candy and not like its namesake city in California. Location: Carmel, Hamilton County. Chapter: *Hoosier Places.*

Welcome to "Stoplight City" should be the sign greeting drivers to this central Indiana metropolis. This intersection at Markland Avenue indicates the midway point in the time consuming trek on US 31 through town. Location: Kokomo, Howard County. Chapter: *Hoosier Places.*

Although most of the IUB campus is adorned with traditional old-world stone buildings, one wonders where they found the former East German architect to design this Soviet Era-esque concrete apartment building. Location: Tulip Tree Apartments, Indiana University, Bloomington, Monroe County. Chapter: *Hoosier Education.*

This photo shows the simple, classic, redbrick style of Music Hall on the campus of the "salt mines," a term my Boilermaker father used for this prestigious institution of higher learning. Location: Purdue University, West Lafayette, Tippecanoe County. Chapter: *Hoosier Education.*

Although ski resorts or snow covered mountains are quite scarce in Indiana, A-frame houses, such as this one nestled among woods, demonstrates a popular Hoosieritis architectural style. Location: Just north of Lafayette, Tippecanoe County. Chapter: *More Hoosieritis.*

This old Farmall tractor is an example of a common Hoosieritis front yard decorative item, and it's for sale too. Location: Dearborn County. Chapter: *More Hoosieritis.*

Because of Hoosieritis, every Indiana native instinctively knows this image, the altar of the State religion. Although this hoop looks a bit crooked and in need of repair, it stands proudly awaiting the shooting of the sacred sphere. Location: The author's front yard in Bright, Dearborn County. Chapter: *Hoosier Values.*

Entrance to one of the Indiana's largest gaming establishments, inviting all that enter to empty their wallets for a chance for a million! Location: Argosy Casino, Lawrenceburg, Dearborn County. Chapter: *Hoosier Values.*

Its fate unsure, the former Seagram Distillery, is considered to be the largest in the world, producing everything from wine coolers to whiskey in abundance. I wonder if there's a secret pipeline running across US 50 into the Argosy Casino. Location: Lawrenceburg, Dearborn County. Chapter: *Hoosier Values.*

My uncle's backyard, revealing his very serious case of Hoosieritis. Question: Is this a shrine to the "Hoosier State Car" or just another automobile junkyard? You decide. These old Studebaker cars have certainly seen better days. The "Fred Flinstone" car is the one in the middle. Location: Not to be named residence in Indianapolis, Marion County. Chapter: *More Hoosieritis.*

The author, standing next to his uncle's '63 Studebaker Cruiser, the "Hoosier State Car." Location: In front of the Studebaker Homestead, Dune Acres, Porter County. Chapter: *More Hoosieritis.*

Additional Photos*

Grave of movie star, James Dean, who was tragicly killed in an automobile accident in Cholame, California. Location: Park Cemetery, Fairmount, Grant County. Chapter: *Hoosier Identity.*

*Photos added to 2020 Edition.

The author at Lake Michigan with the Chicago skyline looming in the background. Location: Whiting Beach, Whiting, Lake County. Chapter: *Not Really Hoosier.*

Entrance to Indiana Beach amusement park, opened in 1926. Sadly, it is scheduled to close permanently in 2020. Location: Lake Shafer, Monticello, White County. Chapter: *Hoosier Places.*

Statue of Liberty replica, erected by the St. Joseph County Boy Scouts in 1951, one of hundreds erected in towns all over the United States from 1949-52. Height: 8 ½ ft (2.6 m). Location: St. Joseph County Courthouse, South Bend, St. Joseph County. Chapter: Not mentioned in the *Hoosieritis*.

The Indiana State Tree, the Tulip Tree or Tulip Poplar, member of the magnolia family. *Liriodendron tulipifera.* Stock photo from Amazon.com. Chapter: *Hoosier State Tree.*

Statues to suit your fancy available at this roadside business along US 31 was once PK Distributors, now Pipe Creek Mercantile (antique store), Location: Miami County. Chapter: *More Hoosieritis – Hoosier Front Yards.*

West Side Liquor Store, known for its great selection and low prices (4.6 on Google reviews). The shadow in the photo is actually in the State of Ohio. Location: Stateline Road, West Harrison, Dearborn County. Chapter: *Hoosier Values.*

The Whitewater Canal, built between 1836 and 1847, went from Lawrenceburg to Hagerstown, a distance of seventy-six miles. Boat rides are available on the Ben Franklin. Location: Metamora, Franklin County. Chapter: Not mentioned in *Hoosieritis*.

The Indiana "industrial" beach scene on Lake Michigan. NIPSCO (Northern Indiana Public Service Company) electric power plant smokestack and Arcelor-Mittal steel mill in the background. Location: Dune Acres, Porter County. Chapter: *Not Really Hoosier.*

Misty morning view from Hesitation Point of the "Little Smokies." Elevation: 998 feet. Location: Brown County State Park, Brown County. Chapter: Not mentioned in *Hoosieritis.*

Towering a nose bleeding 140 feet* above Lake Michigan, Mount Baldy, a moving sand dune. In 2013 a young boy was swallowed up by a hole that opened up on it – he survived, but the mountain is restricted to ranger-led hikes now. Elevation: 718 feet (219 meters). Stock photo from Indiana Public Media. Location: Indiana Dunes National Park, La Porte County. Chapter: *Hoosier National Park.*

*2012 measurement

Hoosier Hill is the highest point above sea level in the State of Indiana. Elevation: 1,257 feet (383 meters). The hill sits on private property in a forested area surrounded by farmland. In 2016 this boulder was put in place because the sign marking the spot was frequently stolen. Stock photo from The Peak Seeker. Location: Eleven miles north of Richmond on Elliot Road, Wayne County. Chapter: *More Hoosieritis*.

Not Colorado, or Utah, or California, but Perfect North Slopes ski resort, the longest ski slope in Indiana with a 400-foot vertical drop. Nick Goepper, Bronze medal winner at 2014 Winter Olympics (Sochi, Russia) and 2018 silver medal winner at 2018 Winter Olympics (Pyeongchang, South Korea) in men's slopestyle skiing, learned his craft at Perfect North Slopes. My son, Danny, went to school with him. Photo from Perfect North Slopes Facebook page. Location: Lawrenceburg, Dearborn County. Chapter: *Hoosier Values.*

Further Hoosieritis Reading

The Rivalry: Indiana and Purdue and the History of Their Old Oaken Bucket Battles 1925-2002, by Robert D. Arnold, Author House.

Indiana Curiosities: Quirky Characters, Roadside Oddities & Other Offbeat Stuff, by Dick Wolfsie, Globe Pequot Press.

Indiana: Off the Beaten Path, by Phyllis Thomas, Globe Pequot Press.

Oddball Indiana: A Guide to Some Really Strange Places, by Jerome Pohlen, Chicago Review Press.

About the Author

Alden Studebaker is an Indiana native, and spent his early childhood years living along the shore of Lake Michigan in the village of Dune Acres until his family moved to Honolulu, Hawaii when he was ten years old. He has a BA degree in religion from Western Michigan University, is an ordained minister, and the author of three other books, *Wisdom for a Lifetime in the 21st Century – How to Get the Bible Off the Shelf and into Your Hands*, a Bible handbook for progressive spiritual seekers, and two novels, *The Grid* and *The Fault*. For further information on his books logon to: https://aldenstudebaker.com

9 798683 851903